Primary Source Accounts of the

Vietnam War

KIM A. O'CONNELL

MyReportLinks.com Books

an imprint of

 Enslow Publishers, Inc. E

Box 398, 40 Industrial Road
Berkeley Heights, NJ 07922
USA

To my father, for inspiring me to "proceed on,"
and to Eric, for joining me on the journey.

MyReportLinks.com Books, an imprint of Enslow Publishers, Inc. MyReportLinks®
is a registered trademark of Enslow Publishers, Inc.

Library of Congress Cataloging-in-Publication Data

O'Connell, Kim A.
  Primary source accounts of the Vietnam War / Kim A. O'Connell.
      p. cm. — (America's wars through primary sources)
  Includes bibliographical references and index.
  ISBN-10: 1-59845-001-8
  1. Vietnamese Conflict, 1961–1975—Sources—Juvenile literature. I. Title. II. Series.
  DS557.4.O25 2006
  959.704'3—dc22

                                    2005018908

ISBN-13: 978-1-59845-001-9

Printed in the United States of America

10 9 8 7 6 5 4 3 2

To Our Readers:
Through the purchase of this book, you and your library gain access to the Report Links that specifically
back up this book.

The Publisher will provide access to the Report Links that back up this book and will keep these Report
Links up to date on **www.myreportlinks.com** for five years from the book's first publication date.

We have done our best to make sure all Internet addresses in this book were active and appropriate when
we went to press. However, the author and the Publisher have no control over, and assume no liability
for, the material available on those Internet sites or on other Web sites they may link to.

The usage of the MyReportLinks.com Books Web site is subject to the terms and conditions stated on the
Usage Policy Statement on **www.myreportlinks.com.**

A password may be required to access the Report Links that back up this book. The password is found
on the bottom of page 4 of this book.

Any comments or suggestions can be sent by e-mail to comments@myreportlinks.com or to the address
on the back cover.

♻ Enslow Publishers, Inc., is committed to printing our books on recycled paper. The paper in every
book contains 10% to 30% post-consumer waste (PCW). The cover board on the outside of each book
contains 100% PCW. Our goal is to do our part to help young people and the environment too!

Photo Credits: American Rhetoric, p. 33; AP/Wide World Photos, pp. 1, 111; BBC News, pp. 85, 95;
CNN, p. 56; David Longstreath, AP/Wide World Photos, p. 65; Enslow Publishers, Inc., pp. 8, 24; Library
of Congress, p. 58; Lyndon Baines Johnson Library and Museum, p. 97; MyReportLinks.com Books, p. 4;
National Archives and Records Administration, pp. 3, 9, 14, 16, 18, 26, 31, 34, 37, 40, 41, 44, 51, 54,
60, 75, 79, 81, 87, 91, 101, 106, 108; National Geographic Society, p. 63; Ohio State University, p. 43;
PBS, pp. 12, 53, 68, 72, 93, 109; Rick Merron, AP/Wide World Photos, p. 10; Ruth Fremson, AP/Wide
World Photos, p. 49; Sandra Wittman, p. 76; Texas Tech University, p. 46; The *New York Times,* pp. 71,
99; *Time Asia,* p. 21; U.S. Centennial of Flight Commission, p. 67; United States Embassy, Hanoi, p. 113;
United States Military Academy, p. 27; University of Illinois, p. 38; University of Northern Iowa, p. 42;
University of Wisconsin, p. 103; Vassar College, p. 22; Vietnam Veterans Oral History and Folklore
Project, pp. 83, 89; Yale Law School, p. 29.

Cover Photo: AP/Wide World Photos.

Every effort has been made to locate all copyright holders of material used in this book. If any errors or
omissions have occurred, please contact us at www.myreportlinks.com. We will try to make corrections
in future editions.

CONTENTS

About MyReportLinks.com Books 4

What Are Primary Sources? 5

Time Line of the Vietnam War 6

Major Battles Map 8

1 ▶ **Dispatches From the Tet Offensive** 9

2 ▶ **A Brief History of the Vietnam War** 18

3 ▶ **Soldiers' Stories: The Words of
      Americans and the South Vietnamese** 44

4 ▶ **Soldiers' Stories: The Words of
      the North Vietnamese** 62

5 ▶ **Dreaming of Peace:
      Other Voices Speak Out** 72

6 ▶ **"Blowin' in the Wind": The War in Song** . . . 83

7 ▶ **Front Lines, Front Page:
      Press Coverage of the War** 93

8 ▶ **To Everything, There Is a Season** 105

Report Links 116

Glossary 118

Chapter Notes 120

Further Reading 125

Index 126

MyReportLinks.com Books
Great Books, Great Links, Great for Research!

The Internet sites featured in this book can save you hours of research time. These Internet sites—we call them **"Report Links"**—are constantly changing, but we keep them up to date on our Web site.

When you see this "Approved Web Site" logo, you will know that we are directing you to a great Internet site that will help you with your research.

Give it a try! Type http://www.myreportlinks.com into your browser, click on the series title and enter the password, then click on the book title, and scroll down to the Report Links listed for this book.

The Report Links will bring you to great source documents, photographs, and illustrations. MyReportLinks.com Books save you time, feature Report Links that are kept up to date, and make report writing easier than ever! A complete listing of the Report Links can be found on pages 116–117 at the back of the book.

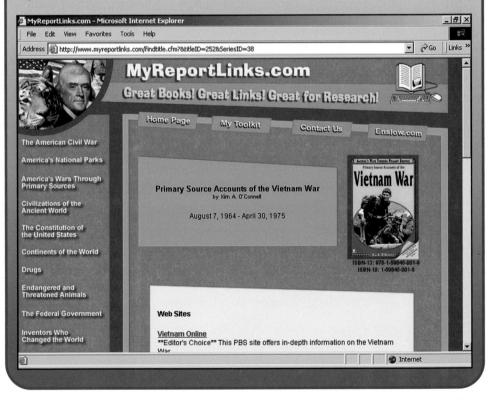

Please see "To Our Readers" on the copyright page for important information about this book, the MyReportLinks.com Web site, and the Report Links that back up this book.

Please enter PVW2980 if asked for a password.

WHAT ARE PRIMARY SOURCES?

January 1968

*My morale is not the best because my best buddy was killed the day before yesterday. . . .
I think with all the death and destruction I have seen in the past week I have aged greatly.
I feel like an old man now.*

— Marine Corporal Kevin Macaulay, in a letter to his mother

The young Marine who wrote these words never dreamed that they would be read by anyone but his family. They were not intended to be read as a history of the Vietnam War. But his words—and the words of others that have come down to us through scholars or were saved over generations by family members—are unique resources. Historians call such writings primary source documents. As you read this book, you will find other primary source accounts of the war written by the men and women who fought it. Their letters home reflect their thoughts, their dreams, their fears, and their longing for loved ones. Some of them speak of the excitement of battle, while others mention the everyday boredom of day-to-day life in camp.

But the story of a war is not only the story of the men and women in service. This book also contains diary entries, newspaper accounts, official documents, speeches, and songs of the war years. They reflect the opinions of those who were not in battle but who were still affected by the war. All of these things as well as photographs and art can be considered primary sources—they were created by people who participated in, witnessed, or were affected by the events of the time.

Many of these sources, such as letters and diaries, are a reflection of personal experience. Others, such as newspaper accounts, reflect the mood of the time as well as the opinions of the papers' editors. All of them give us a unique insight into history as it happened. But it is also important to keep in mind that each source reflects its author's biases, beliefs, and background. Each is still someone's interpretation of an event.

Some of the primary sources in this book will be easy to understand; others may not. Their authors were products of different backgrounds and levels of education. So as you read their words, you will see that some of those words may be spelled differently than we would spell them. And some of their stories may be written without the kinds of punctuation you are used to seeing. Each source has been presented as it was originally written, but wherever a word or phrase is unclear or might be misunderstood, an explanation has been added.

TIME LINE OF THE VIETNAM WAR

1945—Ho Chi Minh forms a provisional government in Vietnam following the surrender of Japan to the Allies at the end of World War II. (Vietnam, which had been under French rule, was occupied by the Japanese during the war.)

1946—Indochina War begins between the Democratic Republic of Vietnam and the French. The United States sends $15 million in military aid to the French.

1954—Indochina War between France and Vietnam ends with the French defeat at the Battle of Dien Bien Phu, ending one hundred years of French colonial rule.

—International Geneva Conference divides Vietnam at the 17th parallel—the Democratic Republic of North Vietnam, governed by the Communist party under Ho Chi Minh, and the Republic of South Vietnam, led by Ngo Dinh Diem and backed by the United States and other Western nations.

—United States president Dwight Eisenhower, fearing the spread of communism in Southeast Asia, offers to help the South Vietnamese.

1955—South Vietnam's president Diem rejects the Geneva Accords and refuses to hold elections. The Communist powers of China and the former Soviet Union pledge to send more financial support to North Vietnam.

1956—American military advisors assume responsibility for training South Vietnamese forces.

1960—NOVEMBER: John Fitzgerald Kennedy is elected president of the United States.

—DECEMBER: The North Vietnamese government forms the pro-Communist National Liberation Front for South Vietnam and begins a series of attacks against military targets.

1961—MAY: President Kennedy sends 100 Special Forces troops to Vietnam. They are trained in guerrilla warfare.

—DECEMBER: Secretary of State Dean Rusk warns that the government of South Vietnam is in danger of falling to the North.

1962—More American advisors and military support are sent to South Vietnam. When Communists move into the neighboring country of Laos in May, the United States sends 5,000 Marines and 50 fighter jets to Thailand.

1963—NOVEMBER: South Vietnam's president Diem is overthrown by generals in the South Vietnamese Army, with the United States' approval. Diem and his brother are shot and killed.

—President Kennedy is assassinated, and Vice President Lyndon Baines Johnson becomes president. By year's end, more than 16,000 military advisors are in Vietnam.

1964—AUGUST 2: Gulf of Tonkin incident: North Vietnamese PT boats are alleged to have fired torpedoes at the USS *Maddox,* an American destroyer, in the Tonkin Gulf. A second, though highly disputed, attack is alleged to take place on August 4.

—AUGUST 7: Congress passes the Gulf of Tonkin Resolution, giving President Johnson the power to wage war against the North Vietnamese.

1965—Operation Rolling Thunder begins three years of American bombing raids on North Vietnam.

—First American combat troops arrive at Da Nang.

—First major battle of the Vietnam War takes place in the Ia Drang Valley.

1966—South Vietnamese troops defend Hue and Da Nang.

1967—Nguyen Van Thieu elected president of South Vietnam.

—Martin Luther King, Jr., speaks out against the war.

1968—JANUARY: North Vietnamese launch Tet Offensive.

—United States and South Vietnamese forces recapture the city of Hue, which had been seized during the Tet Offensive.

—MARCH 16: Massacre at My Lai.

—Antiwar protests in the United States erupt throughout the summer.

1969—Newly elected president Richard Nixon begins secret bombing of Communist bases in Cambodia.

—Ho Chi Minh dies.

—Protesters stage a massive antiwar demonstration in Washington, D.C.

1970—APRIL: American and South Vietnamese troops invade Cambodia.

—MAY 4: National Guardsmen fire on a crowd of student antiwar protesters at Kent State University, in Ohio, killing four students.

—United States troops begin to withdraw from Vietnam.

1972—To force North Vietnam to continue peace talks, the Nixon administration orders heavy bombing in and around Hanoi.

—MARCH: North Vietnam launches Easter Offensive, a full-scale invasion of the South, which lasts until October.

1973—United States and Vietnam leaders sign cease-fire agreement, and the last American troops leave Vietnam.

1974—President Nixon resigns after Watergate scandal.

1975—Communist forces move aggressively on South Vietnam.

—Saigon falls to the Communists on April 30. The last Americans evacuate.

1976 —Vietnamese refugees seek safety in other nations, including the United
-1980 States.

1982—The Vietnam Veterans Memorial in Washington, D.C., is dedicated.

—Vietnam veterans win a lawsuit against Dow Chemical over the use of Agent Orange, an herbicide used to clear jungle growth in Vietnam, which led to serious health problems.

1995—The United States restores diplomatic ties with Vietnam.

Major Battle Sites of the Vietnam War

Red River

NORTH VIETNAM

CHINA

Dien Bien Phu

US Air Raids 1966–1973

Hanoi

Haiphong

Gulf of Tonkin

LAOS

Gulf of Tonkin Incident 1964

Hainan (CHINA)

US Seventh Fleet

Vinh

Mekong River

Vientiane

Demilitarized Zone

17th Parallel

Ho Chi Minh Trail

THAILAND

Hue

Tet Offensive–1968

Da Nang

Dak To 1967

Pleiku 1965

CAMBODIA

Central Highlands 1965–1971, 1975

Tonle Sap

SOUTH VIETNAM

Gulf of Thailand

Phnom Penh

Saigon–1975

N
W   E
S

Saigon

Mekong Delta

South China Sea

▲ The sites in red are the places where, from 1964 to 1975, the major battles of the Vietnam War were fought.

DISPATCHES FROM THE TET OFFENSIVE

On January 30, 1968, seventy thousand North Vietnamese soldiers celebrated Tet, their Lunar New Year, in a brutal way. A war had been raging between North Vietnam and South Vietnam for years. In 1954, after years of bloodshed, the international Geneva Conference had split the country of Vietnam into two republics. North Vietnam was led by the Communist party under Ho Chi Minh, while South Vietnam received the support of the United States and other Western nations.

United States military advisors had been training South Vietnamese

In this photograph from 1954, Ho Chi Minh, Vietnam's Communist leader, accuses the United States of interfering in his country's struggle for independence. That struggle would continue for nearly twenty more years—and lead to the deaths of countless Vietnamese and more than fifty thousand Americans.

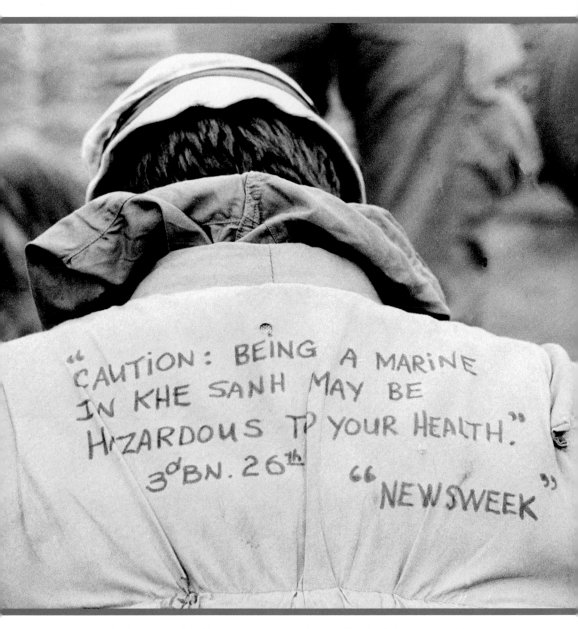

▲ *A testament to the dangerous conditions at Khe Sanh in February 1968 appears on the back of this Marine's flak vest.*

soldiers since 1956, when the French left Vietnam. Large groups of Americans had been fighting alongside South Vietnamese since 1965. By the beginning of 1968, more than five hundred thousand American troops were serving in Vietnam. Fighting was fierce, and both sides had suffered thousands of dead and wounded. On the eve of the Tet celebration, however, the armies had agreed to a truce, or cease-fire, during the holiday. But the North Vietnamese had a trick up their sleeves.

In what would be called the Tet Offensive, instead of keeping the truce, the North Vietnamese Army led a surprise attack. With help from guerrilla forces known as the Vietcong, or VC, the North Vietnamese attacked more than a hundred cities and towns in Vietnam. Even the most fortified places were hit. Northern troops attacked the American embassy in Saigon, the capital of South Vietnam. Another target was the United States military base at Cam Ranh Bay.

▶ A Narrow Escape

Alan Bourne, who was a first lieutenant with an artillery unit of the 199th Light Infantry Brigade, was caught in the Tet Offensive and barely escaped with his life. On January 31, 1968, he wrote to his girlfriend, Chris:

Yesterday afternoon we were given an emergency mission to move about 10 miles to a new position. We got

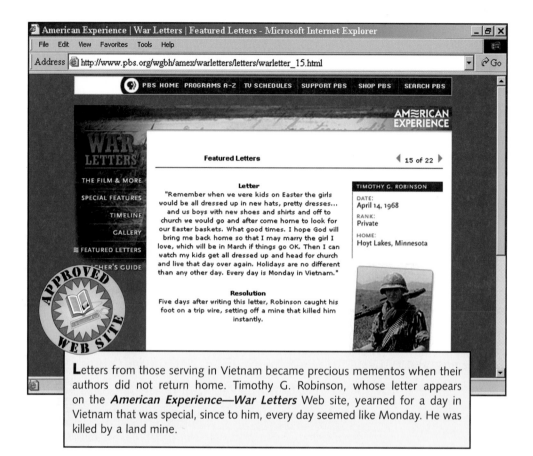

PBS HOME PROGRAMS A–Z TV SCHEDULES SUPPORT PBS SHOP PBS SEARCH PBS

AMERICAN
EXPERIENCE

WAR
LETTERS

THE FILM & MORE

SPECIAL FEATURES

TIMELINE

GALLERY

FEATURED LETTERS

...HER'S GUIDE

APPROVED WEB SITE

Featured Letters   ◀ 15 of 22 ▶

Letter
"Remember when we were kids on Easter the girls would be all dressed up in new hats, pretty dresses... and us boys with new shoes and shirts and off to church we would go and after come home to look for our Easter baskets. What good times. I hope God will bring me back home so that I may marry the girl I love, which will be in March if things go OK. Then I can watch my kids get all dressed up and head for church and live that day over again. Holidays are no different than any other day. Every day is Monday in Vietnam."

Resolution
Five days after writing this letter, Robinson caught his foot on a trip wire, setting off a mine that killed him instantly.

TIMOTHY G. ROBINSON

DATE:
April 14, 1968

RANK:
Private

HOME:
Hoyt Lakes, Minnesota

Letters from those serving in Vietnam became precious mementos when their authors did not return home. Timothy G. Robinson, whose letter appears on the *American Experience—War Letters* Web site, yearned for a day in Vietnam that was special, since to him, every day seemed like Monday. He was killed by a land mine.

there about 6:30 and deployed the men. About midnight . . . we were sitting right in the middle of the boondocks [when] rockets, flares, machine guns, and planes started shooting. The VC got Bien Hoa airport and Long Binh province about 24 hours after I got out! Chris, someone said a prayer for me. . . .

We just had a Vietnamese man come into our position with a terrible cut on his leg. "Doc" took a look at it and said that "gang green" [slang for gangrene, a serious infection that can lead to amputation and death] had set in. We called in a helicopter and had him lifted to a hospital. One minute we're killing them, the next we're saving their lives.[1]

Lieutenant Bourne survived his close call. After the war, he became a real estate broker in New York City. But for him and thousands of other young Americans, their memories of Vietnam—of a war never officially declared and one that became increasingly unpopular at home—would linger.

▶ "The Most Unbelievable Night"

After the first assaults, however, many soldiers were wounded or killed. On February 2, 1968, Corporal Cottrell Fox was lucky to be recovering at the 91st Evacuation Hospital at Cam Ranh Bay. "Cot," as he was known, had been wounded on the first day of the Tet Offensive, but he finally felt well enough to write a letter home to his parents in St. Louis, Missouri:

Well, here I am at the U.S. Air Force Hospital in beautiful Cam Ranh Bay. I've got lacerations of the scalp, a ringing in my ears, a bullet hole in my right arm, and frag wounds over my whole lower body—my left leg looks like a model of the surface of the moon. How did all this come to pass? On the night of 31 Jan. Hotel 8 was attacked by an estimated 400 VC with mortars, rockets, ground assault, sappers, and gas. . . .

It was the most unbelievable night that I'll ever spend. I've never really thought that I was going to die before, but that night I truly believed that I would. It was [something] no civilian and hardly any Marine can imagine. No words can describe it and no one can begin to appreciate it unless he has lived through a similar situation. Firefights and heavy contact are not even in the same league. This is something special.

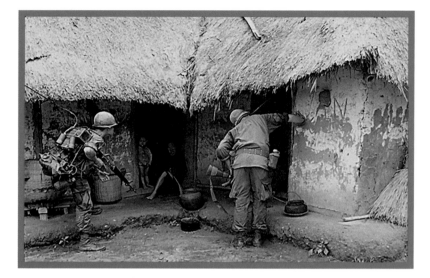

▲ Troops of "A" Company, the 1st Air Cavalry Division, check a house during a patrol. The house and its inhabitants were in an area where two battalions of North Vietnamese troops were supposed to be preparing to attack a nearby airstrip.

I have never fought so hard in my life. I have never wanted to see dawn break so badly.

This was, to understate it, the most intense experience of my life. It has taken me a couple of days to get up the gumption to write about it. I do not write about it happily because I'm very weary of war—although I enjoy it while the shooting is going on. If I could just blow [the enemy] away and then forget about it for a few days, it would be great. I am writing to you all about it because I feel you deserve to know about it and because I know that later, if I make it home, that I will want some sort of record of what happened to me in Nam.[2]

▶ Under Alert

Although the soldiers on the front lines faced the most serious danger during the Tet Offensive, the widespread attack made everyone nervous, even those in support positions. Sergeant F. Lee Hudson III was working with the United States field artillery when the North Vietnamese launched their offensive. In a letter home to his parents in New Jersey, Hudson talked about how his unit kept working to stack up the ammunition for the front-line troops, even as the fighting got dangerously close.

"I know you must be pretty worried with all the action that is going on," Hudson wrote on February 2, 1968:

. . . Today has really been a wild one. Just before noon today everybody was rushed over to the ammo dump. Because of all the firing in the last few days, our batteries are running low on ammunition. So today a rush convoy from Long Binh came up with the ammo and the guys had to break it down and restack it for helicopters. They worked right through lunch and dinner. Now it's eight o'clock and they're still working.

The ammo pickup area is right near our perimeter, and around six o'clock we had incoming small arms fire from Charlie [a common nickname for the enemy]. The whole base is under alert, but after the firing stopped they went back to work again. We're still under alert and this may be on for a few more days. We haven't been able to get any laundry in or out and most of us are wearing dirty clothes. . . . Charlie seems to be everywhere.[3]

▷ An Uneasy Feeling

To some American soldiers, the Tet Offensive was not a complete surprise. Lieutenant Colonel John Gibler, who was commander of the 3rd Battalion, 7th Infantry Regiment, was stationed at Binh Chanh, a small village not far from Saigon. The North Vietnamese Army was acting strange, he thought. He had an uneasy feeling that they might launch an attack on the southern capital. On the night before Tet, he ordered all his soldiers to return to the base. When an officer asked him why, he said, "I don't know; I just want 'em on their way back in."[4]

When the Tet Offensive began the next morning, Gibler learned that his suspicions had been right. Although Binh Chanh was not attacked, Gibler's troops were asked to join the American forces that were fighting in the

◁ *During the vicious fighting of the Tet Offensive, Vietnamese refugees flee Hue, once Vietnam's capital.*

streets of Saigon. By mid-February, most of the VC were defeated, after intense house-to-house combat through Vietnamese cities. In the end, North Vietnam had not won any major area and had suffered tens of thousands of casualties.

"I think the VC made two major mistakes," Lieutenant General Frederick Weyand wrote after the battle. "First, by attacking everywhere at once, they fragmented their forces and laid themselves open to defeat in detail." Second, Weyand continued, the North Vietnamese Army wrongly believed that Southern Vietnamese would join the Northern soldiers in great numbers.[5]

Although the United States and its allies in Vietnam had beaten back the Tet Offensive, the attacks did hurt their cause. Before Tet, many Americans back home believed that the war was going well and would soon be over. The Lunar New Year attacks made them feel differently. In letters, poems, songs, and reports both before and after Tet, Americans talked about the danger, fear, sadness, and boredom—as well as the few bright spots—that were part of their Vietnam War experience.

A BRIEF HISTORY OF THE VIETNAM WAR

On a human scale, all wars are devastating. Soldiers are wounded, lives are lost, and families are torn apart. Men and women are forever changed. But even though all wars are devastating, some are more so than others. Such is the case with the war in Vietnam. It was, in the words of journalist Stanley Karnow, "a war that nobody won—a struggle between victims. . . . a tragedy of epic dimensions."[1]

Other wars had clear battle lines, and American troops could measure their progress by conquering territory. But in Vietnam, soldiers fought over the same ground again and again, never sure

◀Many of the American soldiers who fought in Vietnam were not much older than this young Marine private, photographed during the Marine landing on the beach at Da Nang in 1965.

where the enemy was. In other wars, the enemy was easily defined and even dressed in a recognizable uniform. In Vietnam, American soldiers had to deal with an unofficial army of warriors—the Vietcong, or VC—who laid booby traps and sometimes dressed like peasants.

The Sacrifice

Most American soldiers in Vietnam were young, fresh faced, and often poorly equipped—at least, emotionally—for this unconventional warfare. The average age of an American soldier in Vietnam was only nineteen, a full seven years younger than the average American fighting in World War II. In Vietnam, even more so than in other wars, American soldiers seemed too young to die. Yet thousands did. In all, there were 58,193 American casualties as a result of the Vietnam War, including those declared dead later because they had been prisoners of war (POWs) or were missing in action (MIAs). The vast majority were killed in combat, but about ten thousand died from disease and other causes.

The Vietnamese people suffered far greater losses. More than two hundred thousand South Vietnamese were killed, and estimates place North Vietnamese casualties at about a million, although that figure has been disputed. Untold thousands of civilians on both sides, as well as Vietcong irregulars, also perished.

Arriving in Vietnam in 1967, journalist Jurate Kazickas reported on the war from the hilly village of Khe Sanh. "When I think of Vietnam, I think of the soldiers' faces," she later wrote. "Unguarded, innocent, smiling. . . . No one wanted to be in that distant, strange land, but they did not complain. Some felt it was their duty to come to Vietnam. Some never stopped questioning why they were there."[2]

▶ The Rise of Ho Chi Minh

To the Vietnamese, the war was a continuation of the nation's long struggle against foreign rule. In ancient times, several Chinese dynasties had claimed control over Vietnam. According to a beloved Vietnamese legend, the two Trung sisters successfully led a revolt against the Chinese Han Dynasty in A.D. 40, becoming the first Vietnamese patriots. History repeated itself in the nineteenth and twentieth centuries. France had claimed colonial rule over Vietnam since the mid-nineteenth century, although Japanese forces occupied Vietnam during World War II. During the war, an ambitious resistance fighter and Communist named Ho Chi Minh began to stir up dissent and organized a group of Vietnamese nationalists known as the Vietminh to fight the Japanese. Uncle Ho, as he was sometimes called, wanted to "liberate" and unify Vietnam under the Communist banner.

In 1945, with the Japanese surrender and Allied victory in World War II, Ho declared Vietnam's independence from France. But no foreign countries

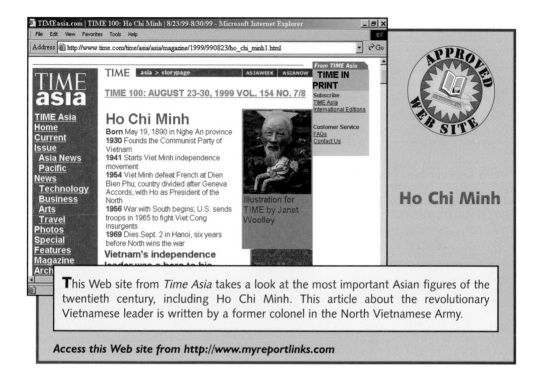

TIMEasia.com | TIME 100: Ho Chi Minh | 8/23/99-8/30/99 - Microsoft Internet Explorer

File   Edit   View   Favorites   Tools   Help

Address   http://www.time.com/time/asia/asia/magazine/1999/990823/ho_chi_minh1.html

TIME asia

TIME   asia > storypage   ASIAWEEK | ASIANOW

TIME 100: AUGUST 23-30, 1999 VOL. 154 NO. 7/8

TIME Asia
Home
Current
Issue
Asia News
Pacific
News
Technology
Business
Arts
Travel
Photos
Special
Features
Magazine
Arch

From TIME Asia
TIME IN PRINT
Subscribe
TIME Asia
International Editions

Customer Service
FAQs
Contact Us

Ho Chi Minh

Born May 19, 1890 in Nghe An province
1930 Founds the Communist Party of Vietnam
1941 Starts Viet Minh independence movement
1954 Viet Minh defeat French at Dien Bien Phu; country divided after Geneva Accords, with Ho as President of the North
1956 War with South begins; U.S. sends troops in 1965 to fight Viet Cong insurgents
1969 Dies Sept. 2 in Hanoi, six years before North wins the war
Vietnam's independence

Illustration for TIME by Janet Woolley

Ho Chi Minh

This Web site from *Time Asia* takes a look at the most important Asian figures of the twentieth century, including Ho Chi Minh. This article about the revolutionary Vietnamese leader is written by a former colonel in the North Vietnamese Army.

Access this Web site from http://www.myreportlinks.com

recognized the new Republic of Vietnam as a valid nation. That recognition would have to come by force, Ho believed. By 1946, the French and the Vietminh were engaged in bitter warfare, and the United States supported the French in what became known as the Indochina War. But the French forces were hopelessly outmaneuvered by the Vietminh forces. In 1954, Ho's army defeated the French at the decisive Battle of Dien Bien Phu, and the French withdrew from Vietnam, ending one hundred years of colonial rule.

Instead of uniting Vietnam, however, the withdrawal of the French raised a concern by Western democracies over Vietnam's Communist leadership.

The Wars for
Viet Nam:
1945 to 1975

A VASSAR COLLEGE SITE

the wars for
Viet Nam:
1945 to 1975

• The Viet Nam War: An Overview
• The Documents
• Other Viet Nam Links
• The Battles of the Ia Drang Valley

America's longest war ended more than two decades ago, yet a number of significant and important questions remain unanswered: What was the nature of the modern Vietnamese revolution? How can we explain the American intervention? Why did the war drag on so long?

Critics of the American intervention claim that the war was unnecessary and immoral and that policymakers in Washington dragged the country into an unwanted war. In contrast, a small group of scholars and military leaders offer an emotional defense of American intervention. A careful examination

From this Vassar College Web site, learn about the wars fought in Vietnam from 1945 to 1975. Here you will find an overview of the Vietnam War, documents and letters, and links to other resources.

EDITOR'S CHOICE

Access this Web site from http://www.myreportlinks.com

Communist societies are governed by a single party in which the government controls the production of goods and services, and all goods are owned in common. By contrast, democratic societies—such as that of the United States—are governed by representatives elected by the people, and their economies are based on competition between private companies or corporations. Soon after the end of World War II, the United States and the former Soviet Union, who had fought on the same side, began a period of mistrust and antagonism known as the Cold War that would last for forty-five years. That mistrust was fueled by each superpower's nuclear weapons, which were capable of catastrophic destruction.

▷ The Domino Theory

In 1954, the fear over the spread of communism into Southeast Asia was given voice by President Dwight Eisenhower. He responded to the French defeat by the Vietminh and France's withdrawal from Vietnam by warning that if communism were to take hold in Vietnam, it would spread to neighboring countries if left unchecked. He referred to this as the domino theory in a press conference on April 7: "You have a row of dominoes set up. You knock over the first one, and what will happen to the last one is the certainty that it will go over very quickly."[3]

▷ The Geneva Accords Split the Country

In 1954, delegates from nine nations met in Geneva, Switzerland, to sign an agreement ending the hostilities between Vietnam and France. The agreement divided Vietnam into two nations at the 17th parallel, but that division was supposed to be temporary, until nationwide elections could be held in 1956. North Vietnam, supported by the People's Republic of China and the former Soviet Union, both Communist powers, would be governed by the Communist party under Ho Chi Minh. South Vietnam, led by Bao Dai and then Ngo Dinh Diem, was backed by the United States and other Western nations.

▷ An Increasing United States Presence

The governments of China and the Soviet Union pledged additional support for North Vietnam, while

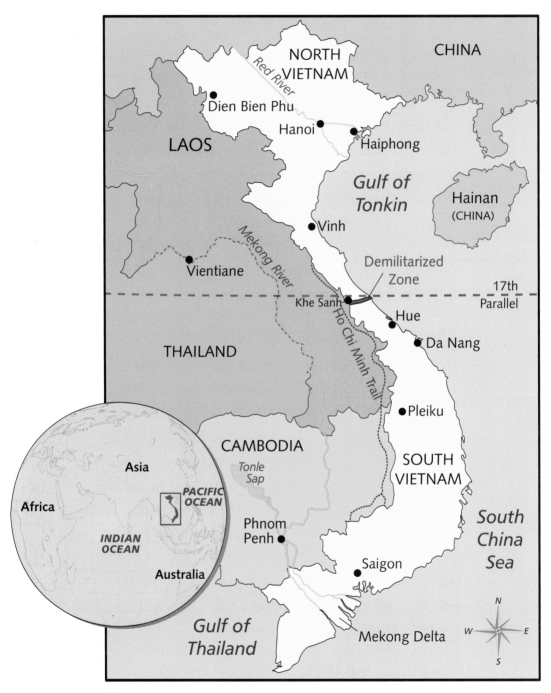

NORTH VIETNAM

CHINA

Red River

Dien Bien Phu

Hanoi

Haiphong

LAOS

Gulf of
Tonkin

Hainan
(CHINA)

Vinh

Mekong River

Vientiane

Demilitarized
Zone

17th
Parallel

Khe Sanh

Hue

THAILAND

Ho Chi Minh Trail

Da Nang

Pleiku

CAMBODIA

Tonle
Sap

SOUTH
VIETNAM

Asia

PACIFIC
OCEAN

Africa

South
China
Sea

INDIAN
OCEAN

Phnom
Penh

Australia

Saigon

Gulf of
Thailand

Mekong Delta

N
W   E
S

▲ A map of Vietnam at the time of the war, showing the major cities
of the North and South and neighboring countries in Southeast Asia.
Vietnam was divided at the 17th parallel in 1954.

in 1955, Diem became president of South Vietnam. The Diem government rejected the Geneva agreement, however, and the deadline for nationwide elections passed. In 1956, the last French military advisors left South Vietnam, and the United States began training South Vietnamese forces. In 1957, the North's Communist insurgents began their guerrilla activity in the South, assassinating more than four hundred South Vietnamese officials. The following year, Communist forces spread along the Mekong Delta, a large area where the Mekong River and its tributaries empty into the sea. By 1959, the North Vietnamese began sending weapons into South Vietnam by way of the Ho Chi Minh Trail, the major supply route for Communist forces. The trail stretched from North Vietnam, through Laos and Cambodia, into South Vietnam. It would become the site of heavy bombing raids by the Americans as the war intensified.

▷ JFK, Diem, and Escalation

In November 1960, John F. Kennedy defeated Richard Nixon to win the presidency of the United States. The same year, the Communist government in North Vietnam's capital, Hanoi, formed the National Liberation Front for South Vietnam, referred to by South Vietnam's president Diem as the Vietcong. Diem, although supported by the United States, was hardly a democratic ruler, and he escaped an attempt to overthrow him in 1960. He

In December 1960, President-elect John F. Kennedy is greeted warmly at the White House by President Dwight D. Eisenhower. The American military presence in Vietnam, begun during Eisenhower's presidency, increased greatly during Kennedy's.

had already imprisoned and sometimes executed those people who opposed him, including Buddhist priests and Communists.

Tensions Increase

During Kennedy's administration, tensions between the United States and the Soviet Union very nearly resulted in nuclear war during the Cuban Missile Crisis, when the United States found Soviet missile sites being constructed in Cuba and demanded that the Soviets remove them. But although the two superpowers avoided direct conflict, they continued to support opposing sides in Vietnam. By the end of Kennedy's presidency, there were 16,000 troops in South Vietnam.

Assassinations

On November 22, 1963, Americans were shocked when President John F. Kennedy was assassinated while riding in a motorcade in Dallas. Many believe that this horrific event set the stage for the violence and unrest that would mark the rest of the decade. Three weeks earlier, on the other side of the world, another assassination also set the stage for bloodshed and warfare. On November 2, President Diem along with his brother were assassinated by some of Diem's own generals. The North Vietnamese stepped up their attacks against southern targets, and the budding war moved to a more violent level—and the United States would soon become more actively involved.

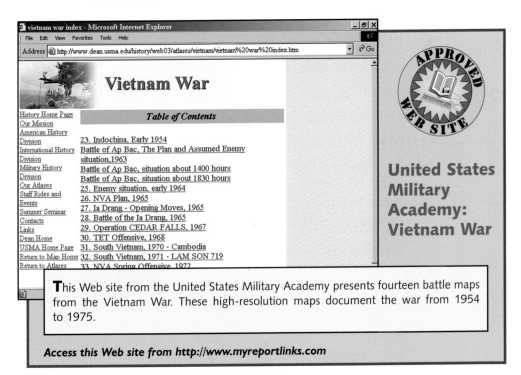

This Web site from the United States Military Academy presents fourteen battle maps from the Vietnam War. These high-resolution maps document the war from 1954 to 1975.

Access this Web site from http://www.myreportlinks.com

The Gulf of Tonkin Incident

On August 2, 1964, the USS *Maddox,* an American destroyer patrolling the Gulf of Tonkin off the coast of North Vietnam, was allegedly attacked by three North Vietnamese PT boats. Two days later, another attack on an American ship was alleged, but that attack is disputed. Yet it was the second attack that led President Lyndon Johnson, who had succeeded Kennedy upon his assassination, to persuade Americans that action needed to be taken against the North Vietnamese.

A Resolution to Wage War

Until that point, the United States government had primarily played an advisory role to the South Vietnamese government. On August 7, after the Tonkin Gulf incident, Congress passed a resolution, known as the Gulf of Tonkin Resolution, that gave President Johnson nearly unlimited power to wage war against North Vietnam without formally declaring war. The text of the resolution follows.

**Joint Resolution of Congress H.J. RES 1145
August 7, 1964**

Resolved by the Senate and House of Representatives of the United States of America in Congress assembled,

That the Congress approves and supports the determination of the President, as Commander in Chief, to take all necessary measures to repel any armed attack against the forces of the United States and to prevent further aggression.

Section 2. The United States regards as vital to its national interest and to world peace the maintenance of international peace and security in southeast Asia. Consonant with the Constitution of the United States and the Charter of the United Nations and in accordance with its obligations under the Southeast Asia Collective Defense Treaty, the United States is, therefore, prepared, as the President determines, to take all necessary steps, including the use of armed force, to assist any member or protocol state of the Southeast Asia Collective Defense Treaty requesting assistance in defense of its freedom.

Section 3. This resolution shall expire when the President shall determine that the peace and security of the area is reasonably assured by international conditions created by action of the United Nations or

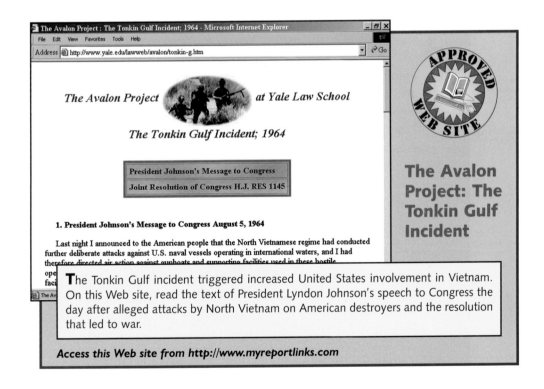

The Tonkin Gulf incident triggered increased United States involvement in Vietnam. On this Web site, read the text of President Lyndon Johnson's speech to Congress the day after alleged attacks by North Vietnam on American destroyers and the resolution that led to war.

Access this Web site from http://www.myreportlinks.com

otherwise, except that it may be terminated earlier by concurrent resolution of the Congress.[4]

At a White House news conference in July 1965, President Johnson explained why it was important for Americans to join the war in Vietnam:

Three times in my lifetime, in two world wars and in Korea, Americans have gone to far lands to fight for freedom. We have learned at a terrible and brutal cost that retreat does not bring safety and weakness does not bring peace. It is this lesson that has brought us to Viet-Nam. This is a different kind of war. There are no marching armies or solemn declarations. . . . Most of the non-Communist nations of Asia cannot, by themselves and alone, resist growing might and the grasping ambition of Asian communism.

Our power, therefore, is a very vital shield. If we are driven from the field in Viet-Nam, then no nation can ever again have the same confidence in American promise or in American protection. . . . Moreover, we are in Viet-Nam to fulfill one of the most solemn pledges of the American nation. Three Presidents—President Eisenhower, President Kennedy, and your present President—over 11 years have committed themselves and have promised to help defend this small and valiant nation.

. . .We just cannot now dishonor our word, or abandon our commitment, or leave those who believed us and who trusted us to the terror and repression and murder that would follow. This, then, my fellow Americans, is why we are in Viet-Nam.[5]

By February 1965, the United States military had begun Operation Rolling Thunder, a massive bombing campaign against North Vietnam. Two battalions of Marines soon arrived to defend the airfield at Da Nang, the first major American ground combat unit to fight in Vietnam. By year's end, American troop strength would reach two hundred thousand.

The first conventional battle of the Vietnam War took place in the Ia Drang Valley in October 1965. The valley was a typical Vietnamese landscape—a dense jungle surrounded by hills. There, the U.S. Air Cavalry Division defeated three North Vietnamese regiments. Despite the win, both sides took heavy casualties, with three hundred Americans killed. It was not long before the people back home began to wonder how high the body count—the number of soldiers killed—would climb.

▲ *United States president Lyndon Johnson, U.S. general William Westmoreland, South Vietnamese lieutenant general Nguyen Van Thieu, and South Vietnamese prime minister Nguyen Cao Ky gather in Cam Ranh Bay, Vietnam, in 1966.*

▷ More Troops Are Sent

The next two years were dominated by both large-scale bombing campaigns against North Vietnamese units and smaller-scale ground assaults. In February 1966, President Lyndon Johnson met with South Vietnamese premier Nguyen Cao Ky and his military advisors to pledge the United States' continued support for the war. Soon afterward, the war began to escalate, or build in intensity, very quickly. By the end of 1966, American troop strength had reached nearly four hundred thousand, and about one hundred thousand more troops would be added over the next year.

One of the largest ground-war efforts during this period was Operation Cedar Falls. The operation, which was launched at the beginning of 1967, involved about sixteen thousand American troops and about fourteen thousand South Vietnamese troops. Their mission was to destroy a major Communist stronghold northwest of Saigon, the capital of South Vietnam. Known as the "Iron Triangle," the region included a massive system of secret tunnels that had been used by the Vietcong. Although the American and South Vietnamese forces successfully destroyed the stronghold, the Communists had regained the territory by the end of 1967. Soon after the New Year, they would use the Iron Triangle as a base from which to launch the Tet Offensive.

▷ Antiwar Protests

As the war escalated, so did protests against it back in the United States. In 1966, veterans of World Wars I and II and the Korean War staged a protest in New York City. Some even burned their military discharge papers as a show of their disgust. The following year, civil rights leader Dr. Martin Luther King, Jr., spoke out against the war as well. King encouraged Americans to evade the draft and stated that antiwar and civil rights groups should work together.

▷ The Pivotal Year

In any generation, certain years stand out, because they were a time when events dramatically changed the course of history. One such year for Americans is

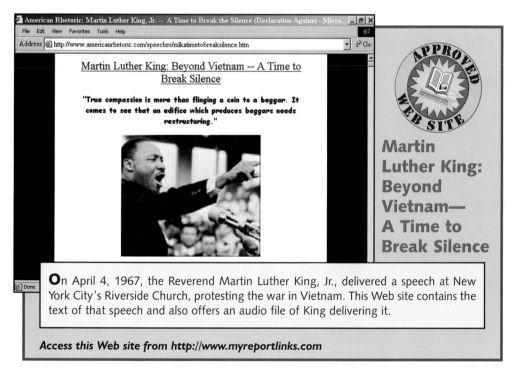

Martin Luther King: Beyond Vietnam— A Time to Break Silence

On April 4, 1967, the Reverend Martin Luther King, Jr., delivered a speech at New York City's Riverside Church, protesting the war in Vietnam. This Web site contains the text of that speech and also offers an audio file of King delivering it.

Access this Web site from http://www.myreportlinks.com

1776, the year Americans declared independence from Great Britain; another is 1861, the year our nation erupted in civil war. Our grandparents and great-grandparents might choose 1941, the year Japan bombed Pearl Harbor, bringing the United States into World War II. During the Vietnam War, the pivotal year was 1968.

In January 1968, North Vietnamese and Vietcong forces caught American armed forces off guard by launching the Tet Offensive. Although United States forces were able to regain control of most areas attacked during the offensive, the northern troops had successfully undermined American confidence in the war effort. Furthermore, the Tet Offensive coincided with long and bloody battles to control

the city of Hue, once Vietnam's capital, and the village of Khe Sanh. The fight for Hue raged for twenty-six days, devastating the city and its people. There, American troops made a grisly discovery of mass graves, which

◀ *General William Westmoreland was the commander of United States forces in Vietnam from 1964 to 1968. During those four years, American troop strength increased from about 20,000 to more than 500,000.*

contained thousands of bodies of people who had been executed by the Communists.

General William C. Westmoreland, who commanded United States military operations in Vietnam from 1964 to 1968, later said that he was aware that the Tet Offensive was going to happen. He believed that if he had been more open with the American public about the attacks and the likely casualties, they would not have been so horrified:

> The American public were caught by surprise. We were making military progress at the time—which [is] a statement of fact. And when the Tet Offensive took place, the American people were not prepared for that, and I assume some significant responsibility for that, and I've made this statement many times. If I would have to do it over again, I would have made known the forthcoming Tet Offensive. At that time, I didn't want the enemy to know that I knew what was going to happen. I did know. I made a mistake in not making that known to the American public, because they were caught by surprise and that was a very much of a negative factor.[6]

The siege of Khe Sanh was the longest battle of the war. More than twenty thousand North Vietnamese troops had formed a ring around the village and the United States military base located there. Hiding in the mountains, the North Vietnamese sealed off all escape routes for the six thousand American Marines and South Vietnamese Rangers that were stationed at Khe Sanh. The two sides fought fiercely for seventy-seven days, and the Marines ultimately held their ground. But nearly two thousand Marines were killed.

On March 16, 1968, one of the bloodiest episodes of the entire war took place at the coastal village of My Lai. There, American soldiers from Charlie Company, 11th Brigade, Americal Division, killed more than five hundred unarmed men, women, and children. When word about the massacre got out in 1969, many Americans turned against the war for good. Lieutenant William Calley, the troops' leader, was tried and convicted of murder by the United States Army in 1971. Although sentenced to life in prison, Calley appealed and was released in 1974.

▶ More Assassinations

But a different kind of war was being waged in the United States, too. On college campuses and in city streets, black Americans were fighting for equality and civil rights. Many of them and other Americans were protesting the war. The divide between political groups—liberals and conservatives—seemed wider than ever. Then, two unthinkable events occurred. First, on April 4, 1968, Martin Luther King, Jr., was assassinated in Memphis, Tennessee. The civil rights leader's death touched off race riots in more than one hundred cities. Two months later, on June 6, presidential candidate Robert F. Kennedy, a brother of the late president, was shot and killed

▲ *In this 1966 photograph from Vietnam, President Lyndon Baines Johnson pins a medal on an unidentified soldier. But the war in Vietnam continued to divide the country, and Johnson decided not to seek reelection in 1968.*

in Los Angeles after giving a speech. Later that summer, the Democratic National Convention in Chicago erupted in violent antiwar demonstrations, and Chicago police, with the help of Army and National Guard troops, responded with tear gas and billy clubs.

In Vietnam and at home, Americans were getting tired of the bloodshed.

▷ Gradual Withdrawal

Although the war continued for several more years, 1968 had been a turning point. In March of that year, President Johnson had announced that he would not run for reelection, so his vice president,

Hubert Humphrey, became the Democratic nominee for president instead. That fall, Richard M. Nixon, a Republican, ran against Humphrey and won. Nixon had promised to unite the deeply divided country and seek a peaceful solution to the war in Vietnam.

Soon after Nixon's inauguration, his secretary of defense, Melvin Laird, announced a new policy called "Vietnamization." This meant that the American presence in Vietnam would gradually lessen, with more and more responsibilities being shifted back to the South Vietnamese. But as Nixon oversaw troop withdrawals, he also began the secret

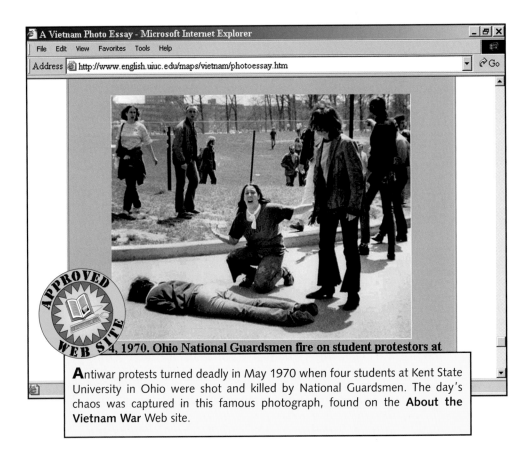

A Vietnam Photo Essay - Microsoft Internet Explorer

File   Edit   View   Favorites   Tools   Help

Address   http://www.english.uiuc.edu/maps/vietnam/photoessay.htm   Go

4, 1970. Ohio National Guardsmen fire on student protestors at

Antiwar protests turned deadly in May 1970 when four students at Kent State University in Ohio were shot and killed by National Guardsmen. The day's chaos was captured in this famous photograph, found on the **About the Vietnam War** Web site.

bombing of Communist strongholds in Cambodia, without Congress's or the American public's knowledge. That bombing, begun in 1969, continued for fourteen months. When Americans learned of the bombing, antiwar sentiment increased, protests grew more heated, and many Americans who had once supported the war changed their minds. In 1970, an antiwar protest at Kent State University in Ohio resulted in the deaths of four students and the wounding of eight others when National Guard troops opened fire on the crowd after some protesters hurled rocks at them. And among the troops in Vietnam, increased drug use, poor morale, and battle fatigue were signs that the armed forces had had enough. By 1972, President Nixon, running for reelection and responding to Democratic criticisms that he was not ending the war fast enough, ordered troop strength in Vietnam to be reduced by seventy thousand.

▷ Coming Home

Later that year, Henry Kissinger, Nixon's national security advisor, negotiated a peace agreement in Paris with Le Duc Tho, the North Vietnamese official who had directed the Vietcong's military operations in South Vietnam since 1955. (Both men would jointly be awarded the Nobel Peace Prize for helping to bring the war to an end, although Le Duc Tho refused to accept his prize.) Under the agreement, which went into effect on January 28, 1973, hostilities would end,

▲ *The end of United States involvement: Henry Kissinger (at right), Richard Nixon's national security advisor, signs the peace agreement ending United States combat in Vietnam. Fighting between the North and South Vietnamese would continue for two years, however.*

American troops would withdraw, and prisoners of war would be released. "We have finally achieved peace with honor," Nixon said.[7] The soldiers were coming home. The agreement, however, which helped Richard Nixon to be reelected, was opposed by South Vietnam's president Nguyen Van Thieu.

▷ The Fall of Saigon

But the war was far from over. In 1974, with the United States taking a "hands-off" approach, the North Vietnamese became more aggressive. Over the next year, the Communists staged a series of major offensives against South Vietnam. In January 1975, they captured Phuoc Long province, north of Saigon. In March, Hue and Da Nang fell to the Communists. On April 21, they conquered Xuanloc, the last line of defense around the South Vietnamese capital.

It quickly became clear to the remaining Americans in South Vietnam—mostly civilians and diplomatic workers—that it was time to get out. On April 29, a fleet of seventy Marine helicopters evacuated more than a thousand Americans and nearly six thousand Vietnamese from Saigon, going back and forth between the capital and aircraft carriers waiting offshore. The next day, April 30, 1975, Communist forces entered and captured Saigon—the

▲ President Richard Nixon holds a press conference in April 1970 explaining military actions in Vietnam and Cambodia.

final piece of the puzzle. Vietnam would soon be reunited as one nation, under Communist rule, with Hanoi as the capital and Saigon renamed Ho Chi Minh City.

▷ The Fall of Nixon

Beginning in 1972 and ending with Richard Nixon's resignation in 1974, the United States had already endured a national nightmare at home with a series of scandals that collectively became known as Watergate. That was the name of an apartment building in Washington, D.C., that housed the head-quarters of the Democratic National Committee. It was broken into by men who bugged the phones of the party chairman. They had been ordered to do so

Digitized Primary American History Sources

Digitized Primary American History Sources - Microsoft Internet Explorer

File   Edit   View   Favorites   Tools   Help

Address   http://www.library.uni.edu/instruction/digitalhistory.shtml   Go

Digitized Primary American History Sources

"The Destruction of Tea at Boston Harbor." 1773. Copy of lithograph by Sarony & Major, 1846.

This University of Northern Iowa archive offers links to primary source collections on the Web. Scroll down to find links to primary source materials about the Vietnam War.

Access this Web site from http://www.myreportlinks.com

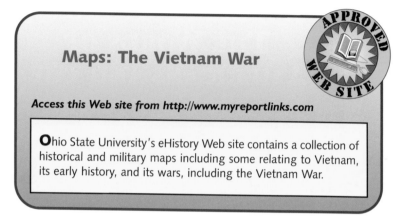

Maps: The Vietnam War

APPROVED WEB SITE

Access this Web site from http://www.myreportlinks.com

Ohio State University's eHistory Web site contains a collection of historical and military maps including some relating to Vietnam, its early history, and its wars, including the Vietnam War.

by some of Nixon's closest aides, working to get him reelected. Nixon's involvement led a House committee, after a long investigation, to issue articles of impeachment against the president. Nixon, rather than facing what was almost certainly going to result in impeachment, resigned the presidency on August 9, 1974. Gerald R. Ford, Nixon's vice president, succeeded him and pardoned the former president. By the mid-1970s, the United States was left to ponder the long-term effects of the war on its policies and its people. After South Vietnam surrendered, CBS News correspondent Morley Safer urged Americans to reflect on the war: "It's vital to refight this war for a long time to come so that we understand just what we did over there, not only to ourselves but to them, and why we did it. We don't understand it yet, and we have to make the effort."[8]

SOLDIERS' STORIES: THE WORDS OF AMERICANS AND THE SOUTH VIETNAMESE

To many American soldiers headed to Vietnam, fighting the war was a noble cause. Their fathers had fought in World War II, their grandfathers, in World War I, and many soldiers felt that they were following in heroic footsteps. To them, the war in Vietnam was a war against the slow spread of communism across the globe. Many soldiers thought the war would unfold the way it does in the movies, where the good guys always win.

▲ *Few Americans were really prepared for the difficult conditions of Vietnam. In this photograph from 1969, American soldiers carry one of their wounded through a swampy part of Vietnam.*

The reality was far different. Vietnam was a war with no obvious front lines. The enemy was everywhere, and no one ever felt safe. The war was fought on battlegrounds large and small. Some units tangled with irregular Vietcong guerrillas, while others engaged with large North Vietnamese Army regiments. Snipers attacked the edges of United States military installations, and incoming mortars and rockets were a constant threat. Over time, it began to feel like the United States was caught in the middle of a civil war.

As the years wore on, it was difficult for soldiers not to distrust every Vietnamese person they saw. E. J. Banks, a former Marine captain, described the feeling:

> You never knew who was the enemy and who was the friend. They all looked alike. They all dressed alike. They were all Vietnamese. Some of them were Vietcong. . . . It wasn't like the San Francisco Forty-Niners on one side of the field and the Cincinnati Bengals on the other. The enemy was all around you.[1]

Over the course of their tours of duty in Vietnam, most American soldiers experienced a wide range of feelings—fear, anger, hate, boredom, and excitement. And many veterans found that nothing in their later lives would ever compare to the emotional highs and lows they experienced during the war.

▷ First Impressions

Arrival in Vietnam brings two adjectives to mind: hot and wet. In the humid heat of Vietnam, soldiers' uniforms quickly became dark with sweat, sticking to their skin. They swallowed salt pills to restore the salt they lost when sweating. Soldiers in the infantry—better known as the GIs—had to carry up to seventy pounds of equipment on their backs, trudging across rice paddies and through thick jungles. Rain was common, soaking everything. The days could be boring and unchanging, as former Marine sergeant William Ehrhart recalled:

> You dug a hole right beside where you were going to sleep and put up a one-man poncho tent. Unless

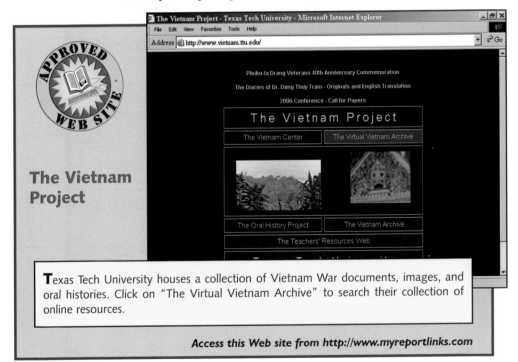

The Vietnam Project

Texas Tech University houses a collection of Vietnam War documents, images, and oral histories. Click on "The Virtual Vietnam Archive" to search their collection of online resources.

Access this Web site from http://www.myreportlinks.com

something happened, you'd wake in the morning with your mouth tasting rotten and your clothes still wet. You'd eat, maybe for a half hour or forty-five minutes, and then you'd be off again, not thinking very much. In retrospect, it amazes me how ordinary that kind of life became.[2]

An attack could change the day from ordinary to terrifying in an instant. Walking along a road, a soldier might accidentally step on a land mine or a booby trap, injuring him or killing him. Walking became a cautious, anxiety-filled activity—not the easy endeavor it was back home. One never knew if a group of Vietcong were hiding in the bushes, waiting to strike. "When you made contact with the enemy," recalled Mark Smith, who served with the First Cavalry Division, "you went from the most horrible boredom to the most intense excitement I've ever known in my life. You couldn't remain detached. Someone was trying to kill you and you were trying to kill someone, and it was like every thrill hitting you all at once."[3]

In May 1968, Cavalry Sergeant Allen Paul wrote a letter to his wife in which he described his first taste of combat:

For the last week we have been waiting for an attack, and last night it came in full force. Honey, I was never so scared in my life. We got hit by 12 mortars and rockets, and some even hit our ammo dumps, which really hurt the battery. . . . We got three men seriously hurt and four others shaken up by the blast. This was my first real look at war, and it sure was an ugly sight. I helped carry some of the wounded away, and boy, I sure hope I don't have to do that again. It was an experience you can never explain in a million words. . . .

I take your picture out quite often and just look at it, because it's such a relief from this pitiful place to see such a beautiful being. I am thinking of you always.[4]

Khanh Truong joined the Army of the Republic of Vietnam as a paratrooper in 1966. A paratrooper is an infantry soldier trained to parachute into war zones. Eventually fleeing Vietnam and becoming a writer, he later recalled the violence of one of his earliest missions:

I joined the army very early, when I was still a teenager, ready to assume all the rights and duties of a citizen. Although my army jaunt lasted only seven years, it left permanent, ineradicable [not erasable] marks on me.

In my first venture out with my unit in a "leopard spot," or Vietcong-infiltrated, area outside the city of Dong Ha, I was accompanied by two paratroopers. When we reached the bend of the foot path, we sighted an enemy. With the automatic reflex of "trained" fighters, all three of us raised our guns, aimed and fired. The man was hit, falling headlong onto the grass; his body went into paroxysm [spasms]. . . .

I hate war.

I detest war. [5]

▲ *South Vietnamese veterans of the war now living in the United States march in a Veterans Day ceremony in Washington, D.C., in 1997.*

▶ The African-American Experience

Black soldiers in Vietnam faced challenges that their white counterparts never had to face, especially early in the war. In the mid-1960s, the struggle for civil rights and equality among races was at its height, but black men and women still experienced racial discrimination back home in the States. Many who joined the military had hoped life there would be different—that they would be treated as equals. That was often not the case.

Private First Class Reginald "Malik" Edwards was a rifleman with the 9th Regiment, U.S. Marine

Corps. He served in Da Nang from March 1965 to June 1966. Private Edwards had grown up in rural Louisiana watching John Wayne movies and rooting for Marine heroes, so he joined the Marines in 1963, when he was only seventeen. It seemed to him at the time the only thing to do, since his parents could not afford to send him to college. He went to boot camp in San Diego, and while it was a less harsh environment than some boot camps in the South, it was still far from easy.

> There was only two black guys in my platoon in boot camp. So I hung with the Mexicans, too, because in them days we never hang with white people. You didn't have white friends. White people was the aliens to me. This is '63. You don't have integration really in the South. You expected them to treat you bad. But somehow in the Marine Corps you hoping all that's gonna change. Of course, I found out this was not true, because the Marine Corps was the last service to integrate. . . .[6]

Edwards's unit was sent to Okinawa, Japan, for more training in jungle warfare before going to Vietnam. He praised the Marine Corps for the physical endurance it taught, showing men "how much of it you can stand." But he was less enthusiastic with the picture the Marines painted of their enemy in Vietnam.

> The only thing they told us about the Vietcong was they were gooks. They were to be killed. Nobody sits

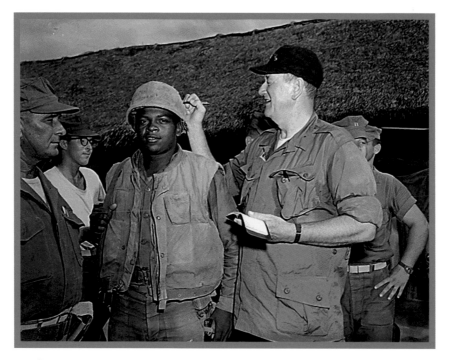

▲ *Private First Class Fonsell Wofford has his helmet signed by John Wayne, who paid a visit to his Marine battalion at Chu Lai in 1966.*

around and gives you their historical and cultural background. They're the enemy. Kill, kill, kill. That's what we got in practice. . . .[7]

Despite the racist attitudes he encountered, he was still willing to serve his country.

What we were hearing was Vietnamese was killing Americans. I felt that if people were killing Americans, we should fight them. As a black person, there wasn't no problem fightin' the enemy. I knew Americans were prejudiced . . . but basically I believed in America 'cause I was an American.[8]

▶ Letters From the Front

Soldiers in Vietnam wrote a lot and often. Writing letters to their loved ones—their wives, husbands, sweethearts, parents, or siblings—gave them an outlet for their stress and anxiety. It also brought letters in return, which were always welcome.

Many letters described the horrors of war in brutal detail. That detail may have been shocking for the folks at home to read, but to the soldiers it was a way to record what they saw and to let off steam. On February 14, 1966, a private named George Robinson admitted that the war had changed his "whole outlook on life. . . . Any combat GI that comes here doesn't leave the same. . . . I never had much respect for GIs even after I was in for a while, but since I've seen what his real job is, I have more respect for him than any man on earth."[9]

In January 1968, the North Vietnamese and Vietcong launched an attack on the village of Khe Sanh, the site of a United States military base, at the start of the Tet Offensive. The attack turned into a siege that would last until early April. About a week after the siege began, Marine Corporal Kevin Macaulay wrote home to his mother, who by then had surely seen footage of the siege on the news:

I guess by now you are worried sick over my safety. Khe Sanh village was overrun, but not the combat base. . . . I am unhurt and have not been touched. I skinned my knee on the initial assault, but other than

Battlefield: Vietnam

At this PBS Web site you can explore the Vietnam War, read a brief history of the war, and view a battlefield time line. You will also learn about guerrilla tactics and the siege of Khe Sanh.

EDITOR'S CHOICE

Access this Web site from http://www.myreportlinks.com

that I am OK. My morale is not the best because my best buddy was killed the day before yesterday. . . . I think with all the death and destruction I have seen in the past week I have aged greatly. I feel like an old man now. I am not as happy-go-lucky as before, and I think more maturely now. Payback for my buddies is not the uppermost thought in my mind. My biggest goal is to return to you and Dad and Ann in June or July.[10]

Soldiers knew that the order of the day was to kill or be killed. Some soldiers viewed the North Vietnamese as simply the enemy, but others could not help but remember that these were human beings too, with lives and families of their own. First

Lieutenant James McLeroy reflected on this feeling in a poem he wrote in 1967, called "Ambush." The first, second, and final stanzas follow.

> One night we wandered far and long
> To kill young men who, brave and strong
> And precious to their loved, their own,
> Were coming to kill us.
>
> Aching, filthy, weak, afraid,
> Creeping through the dripping shades,
> Searching forms through jungle haze,
> We stalked those men as prey. . . .
>
> How can we ever "know we're right,"
> Lost in the dark, primeval Night?
> Must we kill them, as beasts must fight,
> Until the Earth is torn? [11]

▲ *These Marines erected a sign that spoke volumes about their living conditions in 1968 Vietnam: "Home Is Where You Dig."*

Thoughts of Home

Even in the jungles of Vietnam, thoughts of home and the loved ones left behind were never far away. Most who served could not wait to get back to the States, yet many felt guilty about those they left behind in the trenches. The United States often seemed like a safe, welcoming place. But when American cities erupted in violent protests over the war or civil rights, or when Robert F. Kennedy and Martin Luther King, Jr., were assassinated, it was difficult to view "home" as any calmer or safer than the war zone.

Specialist 5th Class Bill McCloud wrote a letter to his parents following the assassination of Robert Kennedy in June 1968. "For a man over here to be wounded or killed is expected and nothing much is said about it!" he wrote. "But, [Kennedy] was a man that did not deserve the pain he received from the wounds, not to mention the pain his family is now bearing. . . . I don't mind being in a foreign country or fighting in the army, but I do mind being away from my family and the others I love when problems or bad times arise."[12]

Six months earlier, as arguments for and against the war grew, a young private named Stephen Pickett, from Jackson Heights, New York, wrote a thoughtful letter to his family. He would be killed on a search-and-destroy mission in December 1967, exactly a month after writing these words:

We were well informed here about the demonstrations by both sides. Even though I'm here, I still have an open mind—realizing, of course, that an immediate pullout or anything of the sort is out of the question. It would degrade the heroic deaths of those who never returned because it would mean going back on everything that we have done. There are many here who feel as I do, but we will continue to fight for the country in which we believe.

Saul Alinsky, the social agitator, once said that no matter how much he criticizes his government, once he has left the United States he suddenly can't find a nasty thing to say about it.

I am sure that that is what the most sincere people feel, whether liberal or conservative. That is one of the very essences of our nation.[13]

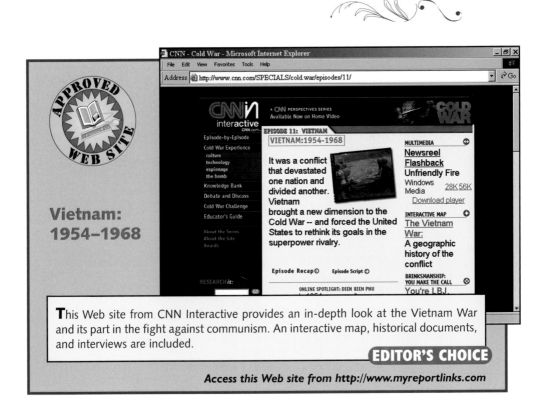

This Web site from CNN Interactive provides an in-depth look at the Vietnam War and its part in the fight against communism. An interactive map, historical documents, and interviews are included.

EDITOR'S CHOICE

Access this Web site from http://www.myreportlinks.com

Toward the end of their tours of duty, soldiers in Vietnam often experienced "short-timer's syndrome." This feeling was characterized by fear about being killed when one was so close to going home—or anxiety about not fitting in back in the States. Whenever possible, short-timers were moved to rear-echelon positions, to ease their stress about their final days in Vietnam. Sergeant John Hagmann, known as "Butch," spent two tours in Vietnam, ending in June 1967. In May, he wrote a letter home describing his feelings as a short-timer:

> You know, when you get over here all you think about is getting back to the World. But when your time gets near, it sort of scares you because you know in your heart that you're not like the people back home. It's a funny feeling to be afraid to go home. . . . And then there's always the way you regret leaving your buddies in this hell hole. We all joke about "Put your time in," but in our hearts we wish we could all go home together. . . .[14]

Butch Hagmann survived the war and returned to private life in New York.

Last Letters Home

The Vietnam Veterans Memorial is a mournful reminder of the thousands of soldiers who were not as lucky as Butch Hagmann. Often, their final letters home were ordinary accounts of wartime life, just as their previous ones had been. Once they were killed,

http://lcweb2.loc.gov/natlib/afc2001001/service/11174/ph0002001r.jpg - Microsoft Internet Explorer

File   Edit   View   Favorites   Tools   Help

Address http://lcweb2.loc.gov/natlib/afc2001001/service/11174/ph0002001r.jpg

In 1964, Denton Winslow Crocker, Jr., was a senior in high school when he ran away from home to join the army. An infantryman serving in Vietnam with the 101st Airborne Division, he was killed in June 1966. The Library of Congress's **Veterans History Project** Web site contains *Son of the Cold War,* a memoir written by his mother.

EDITOR'S CHOICE

however, those last letters became precious treasures for their loved ones. Sometimes, though, a final letter would shed some light on their beloved soldier's last days.

In March 1966, Navy pilot J. G. Pinneker was killed on a mission against a Vietcong unit near Hoa Dong, about thirty miles southwest of Saigon. After his death, a Vietnamese Army captain named Nguyen-Van-Tien wrote a letter to Pinneker's widow, expressing his gratitude not just for her husband's bravery but also for the sacrifices of all American soldiers in Vietnam:

We will always remember the way he made the supreme sacrifice in the manner of a true hero. We grieve deeply at the loss of one comrade in arms who fought so valiantly to preserve the freedom of the Vietnamese people.

To us, the death of Lieutenant Pinneker is highly significant. It brings to mind the daily sacrifice of the American youth . . .[15]

On February 1, 1966, Private First Class Hiram Strickland was killed while on patrol near the coastal village of Bong Son. A month after Strickland's personal belongings were sent home to his family, his buddies in Vietnam found a notebook the private had kept by his bed. In it, he had written a letter to his parents, predicting his own death:

I'm writing this letter as my last one. You've probably already received word that I'm dead and that the government wishes to express its deepest regret.

Believe me, I didn't want to die, but I know it was my part of the job. I want my country to live for billions and billions of years to come.

I want it to stand as a light to all people oppressed and guide them to the same freedom we know. . . .

Don't mourn me, Mother, for I'm happy I died fighting my country's enemies, and I will live forever in people's minds. I've done what I've dreamed of. Don't mourn me, for I died a soldier of the United States of America.[16]

▷ A Hopeful Note

Even in the face of death and destruction, American soldiers occasionally had moments of hope, often because of children. As combat casualties mounted, orphanages in Vietnam filled up with children, the war's most innocent victims. In July 1969, Bruce McInnes joined his platoon leader, Captain Roy Ferguson, on a trip to the Vinh-Son Orphanage. Ferguson had frequently brought clothes, toys, and other items to the children, whose eyes lit up with excitement when they saw him arrive. In a letter to his mother, Bruce McInnes asked her to send him any useful items that he could pass on to the orphaned children: "I'll see that it gets there. And don't be surprised if the next piece of mail you get

▲ Troopers from the 101st Airborne Division play baseball with the children of Ap Uu Thoung.

from Vietnam is a thank-you note from some very, very grateful Vietnamese youngster."[17]

Sometimes, children were the cause of good news from home. In 1971, Frank Russo, an artillery-man, received a letter from an eight-year-old pen pal back in New York:

Dear, Soldier Friend
Hi, my name is Roger Barber. I belong to Den 2 Pack 79. I'm sorry you had to fight in the war. I don't like to fite do you? Please watch out. I'm sending some gifts and I hope you like them. Please have fun.
Your Friend, Roger Barber
Have a nice crismis.[18]

In November 1969, Private First Class Bernard Robinson received some of the sweetest news any man could receive. His wife had given birth to their daughter. He quickly wrote a note in return:

Yesterday, I can say it was one of the happiest days in my life. Hearing about the baby. It was one of the best things a man over here can be told. I wish you could have seen the way me and my friends were acting after we heard about it. . . . Today is Thanksgiving, and I have a lot to be thankful for—a wonderful wife and being able to have a child of ours. I'm thankful to be a father.
All my love,
Bernie, Father of one girl[19]

Robinson survived the war to return to his family.

Back	Forward	Stop	Review	Home	Explore	Favorites	History

Chapter 4 ▶

SOLDIERS' STORIES: THE WORDS OF THE NORTH VIETNAMESE

In April 1976, a year had passed since Saigon had fallen to the Communists. General Van Tiên Dung, who had been chief of staff for the North Vietnamese Army, decided to tell his story to *Nhan Dan,* the official Communist newspaper of Vietnam. Dung's personal history of the war's final days appeared in a series of articles. Demand for the story was great. Eventually, Dung's memoir was published in English as *Our Great Spring Victory: An Account of the Liberation of South Vietnam.*

Dung's book often boasts of the superiority of the North Vietnamese. "From the very first day we confronted the U.S. imperialists, our party evaluated the schemes, nature, and the ability of the Americans correctly, and resolved to defeat the United States' war of aggression," Dung wrote. "Our party knew how to begin and how to carry forward this war for independence and freedom. And now the time had come, and our party knew how to bring the long revolutionary war to a victorious conclusion."[1]

Such accounts of the North Vietnamese view of the war are fairly rare. Those that exist are largely

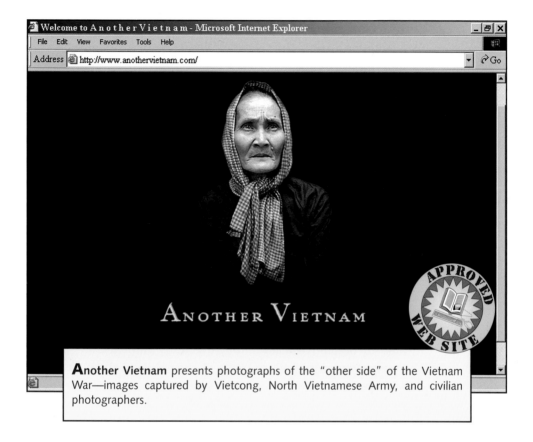

Welcome to **Another Vietnam** - Microsoft Internet Explorer

File   Edit   View   Favorites   Tools   Help

Address   http://www.anothervietnam.com/

ANOTHER VIETNAM

Another **Vietnam** presents photographs of the "other side" of the Vietnam War—images captured by Vietcong, North Vietnamese Army, and civilian photographers.

supportive of the Communist government while dismissing the South Vietnamese government as a "puppet" of the United States. The Americans were seen as brutal imperialists who did not care about the lives of Vietnamese people.

▷ Bombs Bursting

When the Vietnam War began, Americans had both higher and lower expectations of the North Vietnamese than they should have. On one hand, they thought that the Communists had a top-secret central command base from which they launched attacks. On the other hand, United States officials also believed that the United States would easily defeat North Vietnam with America's superior weapons. Both ideas proved to be wrong.

Tran Do, who commanded Communist forces throughout the South, later said that the Northern command camp was loosely organized and moved often. They knew the jungle landscape, and it was easy to stay ahead of the United States troops:

> We slept in hammocks in small thatched bamboo huts, and we held our meetings in deep underground tunnels, which also served as shelter against air raids. Informers in Saigon passed us intelligence, so we were able to decamp whenever the Americans and their South Vietnamese puppets planned operations in the area. Anyway, we could hear them coming, because big modern armies cannot move quietly.[2]

American bombing operations always seemed to be close, but not quite on target. "Still, we had some close shaves," Do recalled. "Once, soon after I arrived, American airplanes dropped thousands of tons of bombs around us, but we weren't even scratched."[3]

Tran Thi Truyen had a similar experience. She had joined the Communist army to work as a nurse along the Ho Chi Minh Trail. As she marched to a location where a field hospital would be set up, she carried a rifle, a shovel, and a knapsack with supplies. The trek was long and difficult, made worse by the threat of American warplanes:

▲ *In 2005, Vietnamese veterans of the war marked the thirtieth anniversary of the end of fighting. This veteran offers prayers for fallen comrades.*

The Americans had denuded [stripped bare] the jungle with their bombs, and there was no place to hide. They would light up the area with flares, then drop bombs everywhere. Each time they flew overhead, our commander ordered us to disperse and dig foxholes, but the bombs fell close, and I shook with fear. . . . Even after the bombing had stopped, I couldn't focus my eyes, and my head ached for hours.[4]

Despite their fear, some Vietnamese have said that the American bombs just made them more spirited and willing to fight.

On the Offensive

Communist soldiers often kept notes and diaries in the field, although most were seized by the North Vietnamese government and never published or sent. Families received only short, formal death notices when their loved ones were killed in battle. Late in 1965, a North Vietnamese soldier named Mai Van Hung began a letter to his mother, describing how terrible the war was. "How devastating and poignant this war is!" he wrote. "It has stolen the vernal spring of our lives, we fledglings who knew nothing except our schoolbooks. I didn't expect it to be so wretched."[5] Killed in action, Hung never finished the letter.

To many Communist soldiers, the United States had no business meddling in Vietnamese affairs. Many soldiers truly believed that communism was the best solution for Vietnam. In one letter written in 1963, a writer praised the villages that had been "liberated" by the Northern army. "My dear brother," the writer wrote, ". . . schools are set up in every hamlet. Cultural activities develop tremendously; song and dance troupes are formed in every hamlet or village, and at district and provincial levels there are Art committees and Art ensembles."[6] This praise was characteristic of a Communist state's support for

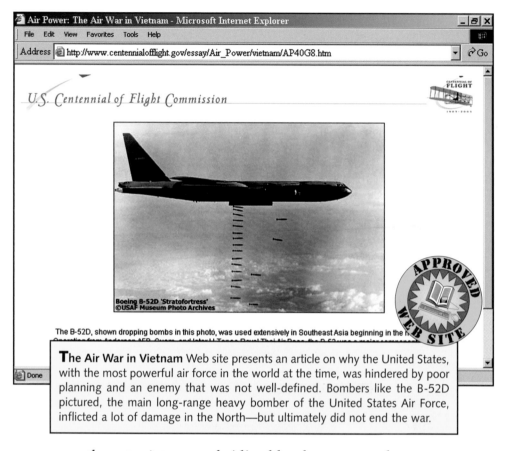

Air Power: The Air War in Vietnam - Microsoft Internet Explorer

File   Edit   View   Favorites   Tools   Help

Address http://www.centennialofflight.gov/essay/Air_Power/vietnam/AP40G8.htm

U.S. Centennial of Flight Commission

CENTENNIAL OF FLIGHT 1903-2003

Boeing B-52D 'Stratofortress'
©USAF Museum Photo Archives

APPROVED WEB SITE

The B-52D, shown dropping bombs in this photo, was used extensively in Southeast Asia beginning in the

The **Air War in Vietnam** Web site presents an article on why the United States, with the most powerful air force in the world at the time, was hindered by poor planning and an enemy that was not well-defined. Bombers like the B-52D pictured, the main long-range heavy bomber of the United States Air Force, inflicted a lot of damage in the North—but ultimately did not end the war.

Done

the arts. Art was subsidized by the state not because art was considered important in itself but because it was a way to show that communism was a superior system.

By early 1968, the Communist army was confident that its Tet Offensive would level a crushing blow on American forces. "Our forces destroyed large quantities of the enemy's weapons and other equipment and crushed several of its elite units," recalled General Vo Nguyen Giap, the chief military strategist for North Vietnam. "We dramatized that we were neither exhausted nor on the edge of defeat, as Westmoreland [the American commander] claimed."[7]

Although the Americans had been surprised by the Tet Offensive, they rallied over the next few weeks. Eventually, the Americans inflicted massive casualties on the Northern army. Communist general Tran Van Tra admitted that they "did not correctly evaluate the specific balance of forces between ourselves and the enemy, did not fully realize that the enemy still had considerable capabilities and that our capabilities were limited."[8]

General Tran Do agreed that the Tet Offensive had not been a total success. However, he noted that it had the unintended effect of turning Americans against the war. "In all honesty, we didn't achieve

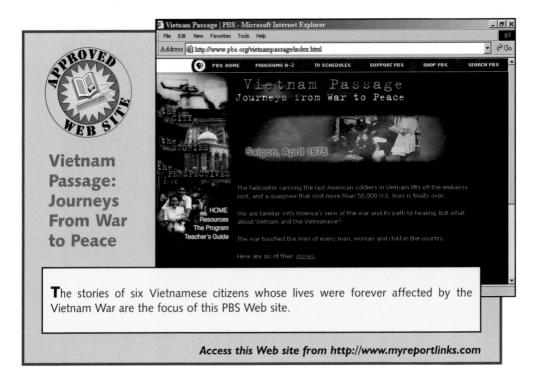

Vietnam Passage: Journeys From War to Peace

The stories of six Vietnamese citizens whose lives were forever affected by the Vietnam War are the focus of this PBS Web site.

Access this Web site from http://www.myreportlinks.com

our main objective, which was to spur uprisings throughout the south. Still, we inflicted heavy casualties on the Americans and their puppets, and that was a big gain for us. As for making an impact in the United States, it had not been our intention—but it turned out to be a fortunate result."[9]

Women at the Front

Women played an extraordinary role in the North Vietnamese Army. They built dams, barricaded roads, and monitored the enemy's movements. Sometimes they picked up arms and fought alongside the men. Le Thi Linh was just one woman who served with the North Vietnamese Army. In 1996, her story was published as *Even the Women Must Fight: Memories of War from North Vietnam*. She told of her sacrifices during the war.

> [The year]1968 was a terrible year. My mother didn't want me to go to the front. But my sister had been killed and my two brothers wounded by an American bomb. I wanted to fight to avenge my family. When my workplace, the Ministry of Communications, called for volunteers, I was ready to go. I was eighteen years old. We walked in a group of 500 young people south, to an area at the battlefield near Hue. There, we worked in groups of five, in our case, three men and two women.[10]

Linh recalled that they were often afraid to cook in the field because they did not want the smoke to betray their location to the American planes. As a result, Linh and her comrades sometimes went days without food. When things got desperate, they even ate grass.[11]

Women often saw terrible things during wartime, which they described in terms that other women could understand. One Vietnamese woman wrote a poem for the male soldiers who were fighting as she sewed their clothes back home:

Sewing machines move quickly.

The forest echoes with the bird's songs.

Our resentment will be changed into silk.

The distant sounds of guns harmonize

With the rhythm of the sewing machines.

We are determined to kill the enemy.[12]

▶ Total Victory

For his part, General Van Tiên Dung remembers that the final battle for Saigon in April 1975 was thrilling. Urgent messages were sent back and forth to position troops and relay information about the enemy's location. The final push into Saigon would be quick and strong. Dung noted how excited soldiers scribbled one of Ho Chi Minh's sayings on their helmets and sleeves: "Forward! Total victory is ours!"[13] Although Ho Chi Minh died in 1969, his

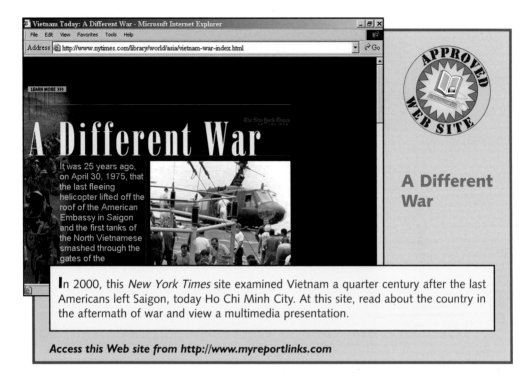

A Different War

In 2000, this *New York Times* site examined Vietnam a quarter century after the last Americans left Saigon, today Ho Chi Minh City. At this site, read about the country in the aftermath of war and view a multimedia presentation.

Access this Web site from http://www.myreportlinks.com

legacy and teachings lived on for the North Vietnamese.

On April 30, 1975, Uncle Ho's prediction came true. As news spread that Saigon was in the hands of the Communists, Dung recalled that Hanoi erupted in celebration:

All of Hanoi poured out into the streets lighting firecrackers, throwing flowers, waving flags. Hanoi, the capital of the whole country, heroic Hanoi, home of Uncle Ho and our party, had accomplished this victory, along with the entire country. Forests of people, seas of people, flooded the streets singing. The whole land turned out in the streets to breathe deep the air of this perfectly happy day.[14]

DREAMING OF PEACE: OTHER VOICES SPEAK OUT

In March 1966, a group of five American Red Cross workers wrote a description of a typical day in Vietnam. Although the women hailed from different parts of the United States—Pennsylvania, Georgia, Tennessee, and Wisconsin—they were united in a single purpose: that of supporting American soldiers

American Experience | Vietnam Online | Reflections on a War | PBS - Microsoft Internet Explorer

File   Edit   View   Favorites   Tools   Help

Address http://www.pbs.org/wgbh/amex/vietnam/reflect/farish.html   Go

AMERICAN EXPERIENCE

VIETNAM ONLINE

ABOUT THE TV SERIES
TIMELINE
WHO'S WHO
IN THE TRENCHES
PRIMARY SOURCES
MAPS
REFLECTIONS
SHARE YOUR VIEWS
TEACHER'S GUIDE

Reflections on a War   return to index

Why I Went to the War   ◀ 10 of 12 ▶

Terry Farish worked for the Red Cross in Vietnam in 1969-70. She was with the 25th Infantry Division in Cu Chi and the U.S.A. Support Command in Qui Nhon. Since Vietnam her jobs have included working in a children's home in Denver, teaching E.S.L. to Cambodian students in Lowell, MA, and teaching college courses. She wrote a novel about Red Cross workers in Vietnam called *Flower Shadows* and a novel about the experience of a Cambodian refugee in America, *If The Tiger* . She has also written novels for children.

NANCY HORTON

Go

by Terry Farish

I went to Vietnam because it was so much a part of the culture I lived in. I went to a women's college in Texas not far from the

Terry Farish came from a family that held the military in high esteem. Her father and uncle had both been awarded the Purple Heart during World War II. As a Red Cross worker in Vietnam from 1969 to 1970, however, she realized that war bore little resemblance to her father's. Her story and those of others can be found on the PBS Web site **Vietnam Online**.

EDITOR'S CHOICE

fighting the war. The group was assigned to the 1st Infantry Division, which became known as "The Big Red One."

In one way, the days were not much different than they would have been back home. After waking early, the women showered, brushed their teeth, ironed their uniforms, dressed, and ate breakfast. After that, the similarities ended. The Red Cross workers spent their days serving food and drink to soldiers, flying in a helicopter to the brigades at the front, and surveying the wreckage of an attack. Back in their tent, which the soldiers nicknamed the "No. 1 Doll House," the workers took their malaria pills, covered themselves with bug repellent, and tucked their flashlights under their pillows. Once they fell asleep, the nurses found themselves "dreaming of the day when our program will be fully operational so we can serve more men better . . . dreaming of the day when we will not be needed in Vietnam . . . dreaming of peace."[1]

Although soldiers got most of the attention, doctors and nurses, relief workers, and civilians all experienced the brutality of war, too, suffering many of the same hardships as the soldiers in combat.

A Veteran Nurse

In the fall of 1966, Winnie Smith arrived in Saigon to begin her tour of duty as an army nurse. As soon as her plane landed in the humid heat of Saigon's Tan Son Nhut airport, beads of sweat broke out all over Smith's body. "Welcome to Vietnam," a navigator said as he opened the plane door. Smith got up to follow him out the hatch. "I stop three feet from the door," she later recalled. "Here the blazing heat of a tropical noonday sun blasts back from the tarmac. My skin feels on fire. Rivulets of sweat pour through my hair and under my arms, soaking my blouse in an instant."[2]

Smith's tour of duty in Vietnam only got worse, as she treated hundreds of patients. She saw all kinds of terrible wounds and watched many people die. She was often nauseated and exhausted, but like so many other nurses in Vietnam, she was committed to her work:

> My perception of hard work, of exhaustion, of tragedy is forever changed. They have become facts of life, the standard by which we live and work, and I wouldn't have it any other way. I'm where I want to be—as close to a combat nurse as I can be, although I wear starched whites [her uniform] and work in an old French school.[3]

Years later, after Vietnam, she felt out of place in the States, unsure of what to do with her life. She had flashbacks and nightmares. People did not consider her a Vietnam veteran, although she surely was. Finally, by reaching out to other women veterans, she began to understand how deeply the war had affected her. On Veterans Day 1984, Smith joined a

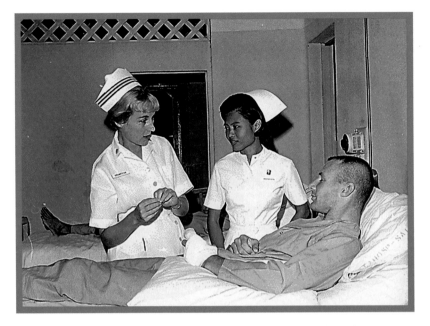

 *Lieutenant Frances Crumpton of the United States Navy, and Nangnoi Tongkim, a Thai nurse, with a wounded soldier at the Navy hospital in Saigon. Nurses suffered many of the same emotional scars of the war as the men who saw combat.*

few fellow nurses at the dedication of the "Three Fighting Men" statue at the Vietnam Veterans Memorial in Washington, D.C. Later, sharing drinks with some male veterans, Smith realized how much they had in common:

We agree that the emotions we experienced that year [spent in Vietnam] were much the same. And we all survived the same way, by numbing ourselves to what was asked of us. They swallowed their fear in order to face the enemy. I buried compassion to face the wounded. Back in the World [the United States] with hearts desensitized and minds numb, we shut out the horrors of the war zone and the turmoil on the home

front, and our self-administered anesthesia has been
wearing off in variable times.[4]

Smith later wrote about both her Vietnam years
and her experiences back in the States in a memoir
called *American Daughter Gone to War.*

▷ "I Get Pretty Upset"

For both soldiers and civilians, it was hard to imagine just how truly difficult serving in Vietnam would
be. As the months wore on, the stress of wartime
took its toll. Bridget Gregory worked for the Red
Cross aboard the USS *Sanctuary,* which was
anchored off the coast of Vietnam in 1968 and 1969.
When she first arrived in Saigon in May 1968, she

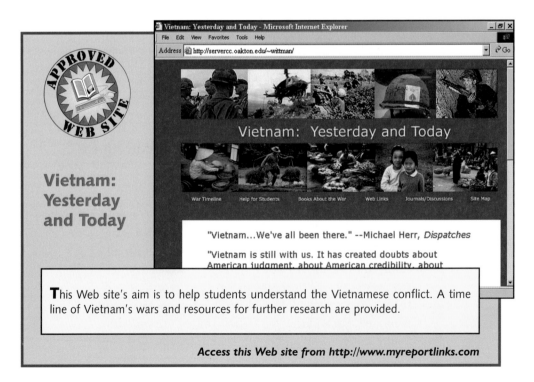

Vietnam:
Yesterday
and Today

Vietnam: Yesterday and Today

War Timeline   Help for Students   Books About the War   Web Links   Journals/Discussions   Site Map

"Vietnam...We've all been there." --Michael Herr, *Dispatches*

"Vietnam is still with us. It has created doubts about
American judgment, about American credibility, about

This Web site's aim is to help students understand the Vietnamese conflict. A time
line of Vietnam's wars and resources for further research are provided.

Access this Web site from http://www.myreportlinks.com

found the conditions in the South Vietnamese capital to be exotic and exciting—even the garbage in the streets and bombed-out buildings. In one of her earliest letters home, which were later published in *Dear Wisconsin . . . Love, Vietnam,* she declared, "I'm having an absolutely marvelous time. This city is beyond belief!"[5]

Within a month, Gregory was all too aware of the painful events that were taking place in both the United States and Vietnam. On June 6, 1968, she wrote a letter after the news broke that Robert F. Kennedy had been assassinated, only two months after Dr. Martin Luther King, Jr., had been killed. She compared the shock of the news to the pain and suffering that she and other medical personnel saw in Vietnam every day:

At supper time tonight, a doctor came in and said he just heard over BBC [the British Broadcasting Corporation] that Kennedy had died. It is wholly unbelievable. I think many people haven't yet recovered from King's assassination and this is too great a shock to comprehend for the moment.

These doctors and nurses have seen so much death and horrible mutilation that they've sort of steeled themselves against it. Wonder if I'll ever be able to do that? In a way I hope so, for the cases we work with are so pathetic I get pretty upset.[6]

By October, Gregory had formed strong opinions about the war—and the soldiers fighting it. In a letter to her mother, she wrote that many soldiers that she talked to were not proud to be involved in "this mess," as she called the conflict:

> There's no patriotic feeling like we're doing the right thing and that the VC are a sworn enemy to be obliterated. The guys talk about it a lot, and few seem the "Let's go out there and kill" type. Maybe it's because they read more, or have more education? . . . The few really gung-ho kids I've talked to are young Marine grunts [foot soldiers] who are usually high school dropouts and have been really brainwashed. They're the ones who get right into the thick of things and do the killing . . .[7]

As her tour of duty in Vietnam came to a close, Gregory's letters home were filled with sad stories. In February 1969, she recalled how a doctor was examining a young Marine when the man broke down, sobbing. When the doctor asked if he had accidentally hurt him, the soldier tearfully replied: "No Sir, I'm just thinking about all those other guys still out there."[8]

▷ Vietnamese Civilians

Several Vietnamese civilians have also written about or recorded their wartime experiences. Because so many Vietnamese men were killed in the fighting, many existing memoirs are written by women—the mothers, wives, sisters, and daughters left behind. Amerasians—children of mixed ethnicity who were

A young Vietnamese widow, carrying a ▷ photograph of her missing husband, mourns at a mass funeral service in Hue in October 1964.

usually born to Vietnamese women and American servicemen—have also recorded their strange and often difficult childhoods. Not completely Vietnamese and not completely American, they often felt left out of traditional Vietnamese life.

Nguyen Van Phoung was born in Vietnam in 1967, the son of a South Vietnamese woman and an American soldier he never knew. Later, Phoung came to the United States and changed his name to Christian Langworthy. Becoming a published poet and author, he reflected on how he used to watch the American soldiers in Vietnam and longed to know who his father was:

They were our heroes, and we were fascinated by their weapons of war. We often imitated the way they walked and carried their rifles. We played war games on the streets with the neighborhood boys. Every military piece of trash that we found became a prized possession: belt buckles, brass shells, helmet liners, or canteens. But the most prized items were live rounds [ammunition]. We spent endless hours trying to fire the rounds, striking the priming caps with nails or dropping them off rooftops onto cement. . . . We wanted to be soldiers. We wanted to march on the streets with the men in the green uniforms. But what my brother and I most wanted was for one of these men to be our father, though our mother told us our fathers were dead.[9]

Beginning in 1989, Martha Hess, accompanied by a translator, traveled throughout Vietnam to gather stories from Vietnamese civilians. She published many of these stories in *Then the Americans Came: Voices from Vietnam*. In it, Hess expressed sympathy for those Vietnamese civilians who supported Communist rule and opposed American involvement. Because of this, some American critics question whether the stories are true or greatly exaggerated. Regardless, the stories shed light on how some Vietnamese civilians felt about the American presence in their homeland. One villager, named Mr. Bao, recalled that some American soldiers sought revenge when their trucks were blown up by mines: "And so, in retaliation the American soldiers killed every family they found in the shelters. They rounded up the women. . . . They threw old people in the river."[10] In another story, Cau Ngoc Xuan felt resentful that the United States refused to trade with Vietnam after the war:

We are very poor because of the war. The Americans don't see how they destroyed everything, and they won't pay their debt. I listen to the radio and hear how the Americans still have an embargo [trade barrier] on

▲ *A Vietcong base camp in My Tho is burned by American troops.*

our economy, and have no diplomatic relations with us. That's not right.[11]

In the final years of the war, Trinh Cong Son, a South Vietnamese poet and peace activist, wrote a poem about the losses that the war visited upon both sides:

Open your eyes and look around here.

Who's left who is Vietnamese?

A million people have died. . . .

Go forth to preserve the mountains and rivers,

Have hope in your hearts for a tomorrow

Looking at this land,

Joyfully cheering the flag of unification, . . .

So many years of tattered lives,

Our people bathed in fresh blood.[12]

"BLOWIN' IN THE WIND": THE WAR IN SONG

Although it sounds playful and fun, the song "Yankee Doodle" was written during the Revolutionary War. War songs have been composed for as long as wars have been waged. Martial songs inspire troops in the field and buoy supporters back home. Protest songs, on the other hand, urge peaceful solutions and question the costs of war.

SONGS OF AMERICANS IN THE VIETNAM WAR-Lydia Fish - Microsoft Internet Explorer

File   Edit   View   Favorites   Tools   Help

Address http://faculty.buffalostate.edu/fishlm/folksongs/americansongs.htm   Go

SONGS OF AMERICANS IN THE VIETNAM WAR
Lydia Fish (copyright 25 December 1993)

Fan blades/helicopter blades rotating slowly above a troubled dreamer, **Jim Morrison's** voice singing "The End"...

Young soldiers, on their way to Vietnam in the summer of Woodstock, marching on board their plane at **Ft. Dix** singing "Fixing To Die"...

Correspondent **Michael Herr** catching helicopter rides out to the firebases, "cassette rock and roll in one ear and door-gun fire in the other," or crouched under fire in a rice paddy while **Jimi Hendrix'** music blares

Songs of Americans in the Vietnam War

The Vietnam War "soundtrack" is often thought of as rock and roll, but the soldiers themselves created songs about their experiences "in country." Learn more about their original works on this Web site.

Access this Web site from http://www.myreportlinks.com

Some of our most popular songs were written and sung during American wars. The Civil War produced "The Battle Hymn of the Republic" and "When Johnny Comes Marching Home." World War I was known for "Over There," and World War II for "God Bless America." More recently, the war in Iraq has produced patriotic and protest songs too: Willie Nelson's "Whatever Happened to Peace on Earth," which opposes the war, and Darryl Worley's "Have You Forgotten?" rallying cry of support for the troops.

It was no different in Vietnam. Many memorable songs are associated with the Vietnam era. Some songs were patriotic and supportive of the war. But the period will probably be best remembered for its songs against the war.

▶ Fighting Songs

The Vietnam War has sometimes been called the "Rock and Roll War" because it seemed to be set to a soundtrack of then-current rock, soul, and folk music. Between the dangers of the battlefield and the boredom of day-to-day chores, music helped to provide some of the few bright spots that soldiers experienced in Vietnam. On radio and television, the American Forces Vietnam Network broadcast news, commentary, and popular music. Whether on base or out in the field, soldiers would bring along their transistor radios or tape players.

During the war, soldiers listened to many of the same songs that people back home were listening to. Some of the most-often-played songs are now considered classics. Favorites included "Hey Jude" by the Beatles, "Light My Fire" by the Doors, "Paint It Black" by the Rolling Stones, and "What's Going On?" by Marvin Gaye.

"The Ballad of the Green Berets" was one of the most popular patiotic songs of the war. The United States Army's Special Forces were highly trained units known for gathering intelligence on the enemy. Nicknamed the Green Berets because of their distinctive headgear, the Special Forces often worked along Vietnam's border with Laos and Cambodia. Author Robin Moore and Staff Sergeant Barry Sadler

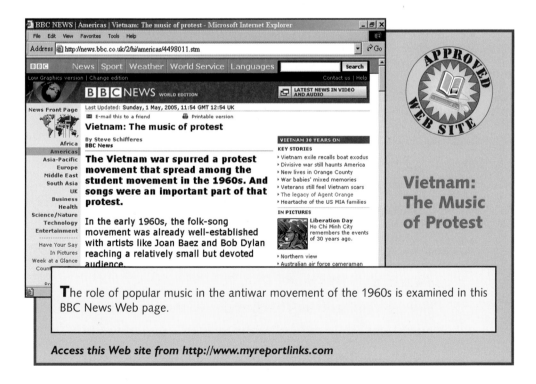

The role of popular music in the antiwar movement of the 1960s is examined in this BBC News Web page.

Access this Web site from http://www.myreportlinks.com

wrote the song in honor of Sadler's fellow Special
Forces soldiers, and it became a major hit in 1966.

American soldiers also adopted rock songs that
sounded like they were written about Vietnam, even
if they were not. "We Gotta Get Out of This Place,"
recorded by a band called the Animals, became a
theme song for many soldiers. After hours at a
Vietnamese bar, soldiers might be found singing the
lyrics at the top of their lungs:

Watch my daddy in bed a-dyin'

Watched his hair been turnin' grey

He's been workin' and slavin' his life away

Oh yes I know it

He's been workin' so hard, yeah

I've been workin' too, baby, yeah

Every night and day, yeah

We gotta get out of this place

If it's the last thing we ever do

We gotta get out of this place

Cause girl, there's a better life for me and you [1]

▷ Peace and Protest

Not surprisingly, as the war in Vietnam went on,
more and more songs addressed the war directly.
Musicians used the stage and the airwaves as a way

to voice their bitterness over the violence and loss of life that came with war. John Lennon, songwriter and guitarist for the Beatles, wrote two of the most popular antiwar songs of the era, "Give Peace a Chance" and "Imagine." The band Country Joe & the Fish performed "I-Feel-Like-I'm-Fixin'-to-Die Rag," and the folk trio Peter, Paul and Mary recorded Pete Seeger's "Where Have All the Flowers Gone?"

In 1969, the band Creedence Clearwater Revival, led by singer-songwriter John Fogerty, released a song called "Fortunate Son." As the war continued, many critics believed that the armed forces were drafting a greater percentage of poor and minority Americans while richer and better-educated people were more often able to get out of going to Vietnam. Fogerty's song title is ironic; the song is actually

▲ *The songs of Joan Baez and Bob Dylan became antiwar anthems during the Vietnam era.*

written from the perspective of an "unfortunate" soldier unable to avoid the draft:

Some folks are born made to wave the flag,

Ooh, they're red, white and blue.

And when the band plays "Hail to the chief"

Ooh, they point the cannon at you, Lord . . .

It ain't me, it ain't me, I ain't no millionaire's son, no.

It ain't me, it ain't me, I ain't no fortunate one, no.[2]

Bob Dylan, who has written hundreds of songs that he and others have recorded, created one of the most bitter protest songs of the Vietnam era. In 1961, on his last day of office, President Dwight D. Eisenhower had warned the nation not to allow the "military-industrial complex" to have too much influence over political decisions. The term *military-industrial complex* refers to the relationship between the military and the companies that supply it with equipment, weapons, and vehicles. Antiwar activists believed that as long as these industries were making a profit, the war would continue. In 1963, Dylan released "Masters of War" as a biting criticism of the military-industrial complex:

Come you masters of war

You that build all the guns

You that build the death planes

You that build the big bombs

You that hide behind walls

You that hide behind desks

I just want you to know

I can see through your masks[3]

"Masters of War" remains one of the angriest songs of the Vietnam period. Yet Dylan wrote other songs that were more poetic and called for peace. Dylan recorded one of these songs, "Blowin' in the Wind," in 1963. The song quickly became an anthem of the peace movement. Before the decade was out, other artists recorded their own versions of the song,

The Vietnam Veterans Oral History and Folklore Project

The Project

The Songs

vwar-l

Related Sites

GUITAR PLAYER
LCPL ST.JEANS
CAD 3-5-5

Vietnam Veterans Oral History and Folklore Project

The aim of the Vietnam Veterans Oral History and Folklore Project is to "collect, preserve and make better known the folklore, especially the folksongs, of Americans in war." At the project's Web site, learn more about soldiers' original songs as well as popular songs of the era.

Access this Web site from http://www.myreportlinks.com

including Joan Baez, Stevie Wonder, and Peter, Paul and Mary. At marches and sit-ins on campuses across the nation, people could be heard singing the song:

How many roads must a man walk down

Before you call him a man?

Yes, 'n' how many seas must a white dove sail

Before she sleeps in the sand?

Yes, 'n' how many times must the cannon balls fly

Before they're forever banned?

The answer, my friend, is blowin' in the wind,

The answer is blowin' in the wind.[4]

▶ "Mother Vietnam"

In Vietnam, the division of the country had a dramatic impact on Vietnamese music and the arts. In the North, the Communists prohibited any music that was not written in direct support of the party and the war effort. In the South, however, Vietnamese musicians continued a long-standing tradition of writing romantic songs about love and country. As the war intensified, however, many songwriters and artists fled South Vietnam for France, the United States, and other places.

Pham Duy, a famous Vietnamese folksinger, was forced to leave the North because of his antiwar beliefs. He wrote many songs including a four-part song called "Me Viet Nam," or "Mother Vietnam," as the war was escalating. The song speaks of dreams of a free Vietnam that endures after the fighting:

A sacred flame so bright

That one and all on Earth shall see.

For Mankind we shall fight

With love instead of might

To build a world that's just and free.

Viet Nam, Viet Nam!

▲ *Music provided an escape for these infantry soldiers in 1968.*

Eternally will shine thy flame!

Viet Nam, Viet Nam!

For ever live thy name[5]

In 2000, after living in the United States for three decades, Pham Duy finally returned to Vietnam for the first of several visits. The Vietnamese government allowed some of his songs to be played again, introducing a new generation to his music. In May 2005, the eighty-six-year-old musician moved back to Vietnam, to live out the rest of his days in the land where he was born.

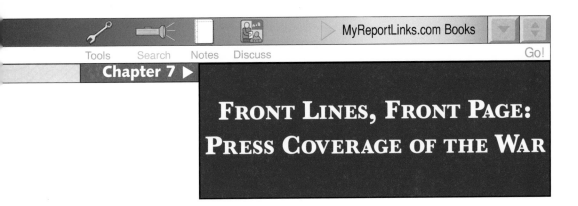
FRONT LINES, FRONT PAGE: PRESS COVERAGE OF THE WAR

For many journalists who wrote about the Vietnam War, the conflict was the most dramatic story they would ever cover. The American media sent hundreds of reporters and photographers to Vietnam to cover the war from as close to the fighting as they could get. Major newspapers such as the *New York Times* provided a daily record of the

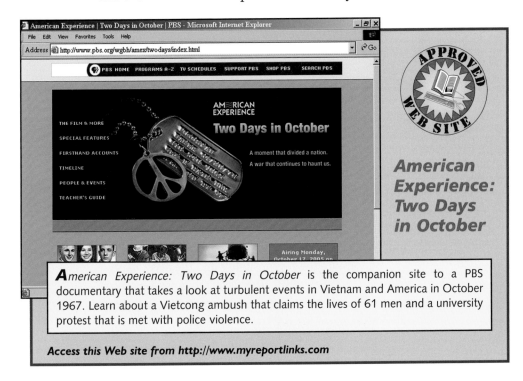

American Experience: Two Days in October

American Experience: Two Days in October is the companion site to a PBS documentary that takes a look at turbulent events in Vietnam and America in October 1967. Learn about a Vietcong ambush that claims the lives of 61 men and a university protest that is met with police violence.

Access this Web site from http://www.myreportlinks.com

battlegrounds—reporting wins and losses—as well as the growing conflict about the war at home. Some reporters wrote stories for wire services such as the Associated Press (AP) and United Press International (UPI). These are media organizations that gather news and send articles out to subscribing newspapers. In smaller towns and cities, hometown newspapers published stories about local soldiers who had gone off to war—and sometimes had to report their deaths.

Edith Lederer was a reporter with the Associated Press when she was sent to cover Vietnam in October 1972. Lederer was the first woman to work full time for the Associated Press's Saigon Bureau. She wrote a letter to her parents describing her feelings about her important assignment:

> Perhaps the thing that is most difficult to explain to a person outside the news business is that challenge of covering a big story.
>
> There's almost a love-hate relationship about it, a feeling that often leaves you with a bottomless pit in your stomach. You are, in effect, writing history and it is through your eyes that millions of people all over the world will see a particular event. There is little doubt that the responsibility is awesome.
>
> But despite the responsibility and the accompanying nerves and anguish, this is what most reporters live for: the chance to be there to cover that unforgettable moment of history.[1]

▶ Newspapers and Magazines Go to War

As American troops landed in Vietnam, American newspapers sent reporters off to war as well.

In Pictures: Fall of Saigon

Access this Web site from http://www.myreportlinks.com

This BBC News site includes images of the fall of Saigon and offers links to other stories about the Vietnam War.

Large newspapers such as the *New York Times,* the *Washington Post,* and the *Los Angeles Times* set up offices—or bureaus—from which their reporters would submit their stories. It was dangerous work, but it was exciting too. Reporters put up with difficult and dangerous conditions just to get the day's big story.

Several reporters went on to write important books about the war, including David Halberstam of the *New York Times,* who wrote *The Best and the Brightest;* Neil Sheehan of UPI, who wrote *A Bright Shining Lie;* and Malcolm Browne of AP and the *New York Times,* who wrote *Muddy Boots and Red Socks: A Reporter's Life.*

Late in the 1960s, reporter David Lamb, who had been writing for the *Oakland Tribune,* left to get a job with UPI. Lamb knew that working for a wire service increased the chances that he would be sent to Vietnam. "I couldn't imagine why any journalist wouldn't want to go there," Lamb later wrote.[2] In 1968, Lamb got his wish and was sent to Da Nang to cover the war. Operating out of a press camp that had been set up by the Marines, Lamb's job was to write up dispatches from the field, which he sent off to a head writer in Saigon:

My pay in wartime Vietnam was $135 per week, no days off, no overtime, no hazardous-duty pay. . . . Covering the war made me happy in an unhappy sort of way. I hated everything about it yet loved the exhilarating adrenaline rush that engulfed me. I thought a lot about death and dying. I felt fulfilled and empty at the same time, lonely even though sharing the life and death of war is intensely intimate.[3]

In the 1990s, as a journalist with the *Los Angeles Times,* Lamb went back to Vietnam to open the newspaper's first peacetime bureau in Hanoi.

Newsmagazines sent reporters to Vietnam too. Generally, magazines such as *Time* and *Life* were less critical of United States government policies in Vietnam than newspapers were, at least at first. In 1965, Hedley Donovan, editor in chief of *Life* magazine, visited with United States officials in Vietnam and wrote an editorial saying that "the war is worth winning."[4] By 1969, however, *Life*'s editors had changed their opinion. In one issue, to illustrate the costs of war, the magazine published the pictures of 250 American soldiers who had died in one week. President Johnson, who often felt targeted by the news media for his policies in Vietnam, said that Donovan had betrayed him personally.

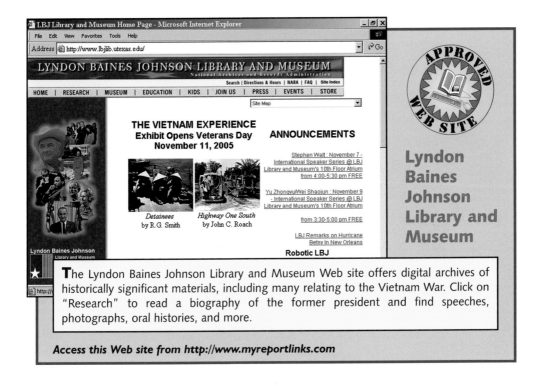

The Lyndon Baines Johnson Library and Museum Web site offers digital archives of historically significant materials, including many relating to the Vietnam War. Click on "Research" to read a biography of the former president and find speeches, photographs, oral histories, and more.

Access this Web site from http://www.myreportlinks.com

▷ Changing Public Opinion

As early as 1965, the *New York Herald Tribune* reported that President Johnson suffered from a "credibility gap."[5] By this, the paper was referring to what many Americans had come to realize: that Johnson's upbeat, positive messages about the war did not match the deadly and disheartening reports from the media. Although it began as one newspaper headline, the phrase "credibility gap," repeated again and again in print and on television, haunted Johnson for the rest of his presidency.

Johnson and other politicians and military leaders blamed the media for turning Americans against the war. But journalists argued that they were simply reporting on the changing views of the American public. At home, average citizens—especially young people—were questioning whether the war could be won. Especially after the bloody Tet Offensive, many people felt that the war had dragged on too long, and too many lives had been lost.

In August 1967, six months before Tet, journalist Keyes Beech wrote an opinion piece that was published in the *Washington Post:*

> The war in Vietnam is not going according to plan. American casualties are mounting. The enemy, instead of yielding gracefully to American military superiority, appears to be more full of fight than before. What's more, he has the [boldness] to acquire some sophisticated new weapons like artillery and rockets. . . .
>
> No doubt [U.S. General] Westmoreland is sincere when he argues that the war is being won, "slowly but steadily." True the enemy has suffered heavy casualties. . . . But if Hanoi isn't winning the war, Westmoreland cannot prove that the United States is.[6]

After the Tet Offensive, many Americans began to openly protest the war. These feelings grew stronger when in 1969, freelance reporter Seymour Hersh published an article about the My Lai massacre, more than a year after it happened. The army had supported the prosecution of Lieutenant William Calley, the officer who led the killing of Vietnamese civilians at the village of My Lai. But the army had tried to keep the story out of the press. When Hersh sold his story to a syndicate—which is like a wire service in that it sends out articles to subscribing publications—the awful truth of the massacre was published in more than thirty newspapers.

Newspapers also reported on the increasing number of antiwar demonstrations that were taking place across the country. After four students were killed during an antiwar protest at Kent State University in Ohio in May 1970, the *Washington Post* ran a front-page story with the headline "Thousands of Students Protest War." Its opening paragraph summed up the anger that many young people felt:

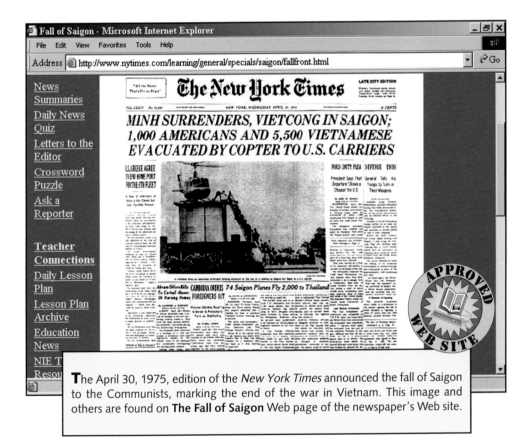

The April 30, 1975, edition of the *New York Times* announced the fall of Saigon to the Communists, marking the end of the war in Vietnam. This image and others are found on **The Fall of Saigon** Web page of the newspaper's Web site.

"Tens of thousands of college students marched, heard speeches, burned buildings and flags, smashed windows and barricaded roads yesterday to vent their outrage at the widened war in Indochina [the region including Vietnam and Cambodia] and the killing of four youths at Kent State University."[7]

The Televised War

Although newspapers and weekly newsmagazines provided up-to-date coverage of the war, many Americans got their information about the war from television. By showing actual footage from the battlefield, TV reporters believed, Americans could see for themselves how the war was going. In addition to reporting on major battles and events, the networks aired nightly updates on the rising number of American and enemy casualties. Over time, the TV networks also began more coverage of the antiwar protests at home.

The Power of the Press

Walter Cronkite was a beloved television journalist who reported on the war as the anchor of the CBS Evening News. With his warm voice and appealing manner, Cronkite was a trusted source. He had sadly informed the nation of the assassination of John F. Kennedy in 1963. Six years later, he would share the nation's pride and awe as Neil Armstrong walked on the moon. Cronkite had been a young reporter in

▲ Walter Cronkite was one of America's most trusted newsmen, so when he questioned the United States' position in Vietnam, his opinion carried a great deal of weight. Here, Cronkite (holding the microphone) interviews an American officer in Hue in 1968.

World War II, and in 1965, he visited another war zone, Vietnam, as a senior correspondent. Over the next few years, he tried to be as objective and impartial as he could about the war.

But near the end of February 1968, after visiting Saigon just after the Tet Offensive, Cronkite felt the need to voice his opinions about the war. In a closing comment on the evening news, Cronkite told the nation that he believed the war had come to a stalemate, with no easy way out:

To say that we are closer to victory today is to believe, in the face of the evidence, the optimists who have been wrong in the past. To suggest we are on the edge of defeat is to yield to unreasonable pessimism. To say that we are mired in stalemate seems the only realistic, yet unsatisfactory, conclusion.

On the off chance that military and political analysts are right, in the next few months we must test the enemy's intentions, in case this is indeed his last big gasp before negotiations.

But it is increasingly clear to this reporter that the only rational way out, then, will be to negotiate, not as victors, but as an honorable people who lived up to their pledge to defend democracy, and did the best they could.[8]

After the broadcast, President Johnson is rumored to have said, "If I've lost Walter Cronkite, I've lost Mr. Average Citizen."[9] Within a few weeks, Johnson announced that he would not run for reelection later that year. The war would become the next president's problem—and the television cameras would be there to show it.

The North Vietnamese Viewpoint

The war received a different kind of coverage in North Vietnam. The main newspaper in the North was *Nhan Dan,* which reported Communist party news. Unlike the United States, which has a free press, North Vietnamese publications had to be approved by the Communist government. Photographs were considered an important part of the Communist media campaign: The North Vietnamese government sent more than one hundred photographers out to the battlegrounds. Generally, they

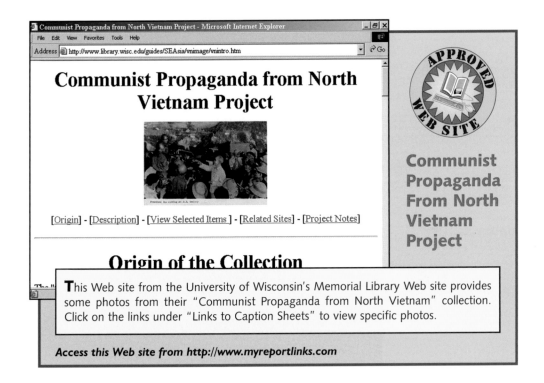

Communist Propaganda From North Vietnam Project

This Web site from the University of Wisconsin's Memorial Library Web site provides some photos from their "Communist Propaganda from North Vietnam" collection. Click on the links under "Links to Caption Sheets" to view specific photos.

Access this Web site from http://www.myreportlinks.com

avoided images of death and disease, focusing instead on civilians or other images that would rally supporters to their cause. Many of these long-unseen photographs were collected in the book *Another Vietnam: Pictures of the War from the Other Side,* published in 2003.

In the early 1960s, one Vietnamese reporter, Pham Xuan An, was a stringer for the Reuters wire service. A stringer is a reporter who is not on staff but regularly submits articles to a publication. Later in the war, An was hired by *Time* magazine—the only Vietnamese person to be hired as a staff writer for an American media organization during the war. Having attended college in California, An felt a strong appreciation for the United States. But he was also loyal to Vietnam. Later, the truth came out that An had been a double agent, reporting on the war for both sides. Although many people were outraged, An defended himself by saying that he had sent basically the same stories to both the Communists and to *Time*.

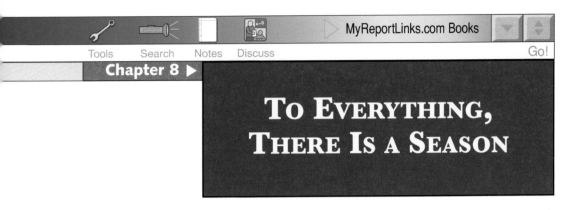
TO EVERYTHING, THERE IS A SEASON

During the Vietnam War, Pete Seeger wrote a simple folk song called "Turn! Turn! Turn!" The folk singer was known for writing songs that protested the war through gentle melodies and catchy words, but not everyone felt they were gentle enough. Radio and TV stations sometimes refused to play his music. "Turn! Turn! Turn!" was also recorded by a rock group called the Byrds, however, and it became a major hit.

Seeger later said that he wrote the song in about five minutes, borrowing the words from the Book of Ecclesiastes in the Bible:[1]

To everything, turn, turn, turn,

There is a season, turn, turn, turn,

And a time to every purpose under heaven

A time to build up, a time to break down

A time to dance, a time to mourn . . .

A time to love, a time to hate

A time for peace, I swear it's not too late[2]

▲ Refugees from South Vietnam flee the Communists in 1975, finding safety aboard the United States carrier Midway.

After the fall of Saigon, it was a time for many Americans and Vietnamese to mourn. It was also a time to move on.

▷ Vietnamese Immigration to the United States

After the war, Vietnamese refugees immigrated to the United States by the thousands, settling mostly in California, Texas, Louisiana, and around the nation's capital. Before 1975, only about 15,000 Vietnamese immigrants lived in the United States. By 1980, about 245,000 Vietnamese lived here.

The United States government had organized temporary camps for the new arrivals, including Camp Pendleton in California and Indiantown Gap in Pennsylvania. The camps met refugees' basic needs for food and medical assistance. They also often offered educational services and religious programs as well. From there, Vietnamese refugees could enter American society by being sponsored by religious, ethnic, or social services organizations.

The first wave of refugees often had ties to the United States government, including high-ranking Vietnamese officers and war brides. Within a couple of years, thousands of refugees arrived, many after crowding into boats and making the long and perilous journey through rough seas, which is why they came to be known as "boat people." It is estimated that between 10 and 50 percent of these "boat people" perished during their voyage, from

Research in Military Records: Vietnam War

Access this Web site from http://www.myreportlinks.com

Casualty figures, prisoner-of-war information, and other statistical records related to the Vietnam War are available at this Web page of NARA, the National Archives and Records Administration.

drowning, starvation, and other causes.[3]

When they arrived in the late 1970s, refugees faced a difficult economy in the United States. Over time, however, Vietnamese immigrants and their offspring put down roots and became a vital and important part of American life. At a Vietnamese cultural festival in Arlington, Virginia, in 1978, Thuy Long commented that she did not mind that Vietnamese and American traditions were blending. "We should learn the beautiful culture of America and keep ours too," she said. "The U.S. is like a garden of flowers. Everyone should bring their own flower to it and enjoy the flowers brought by others."[4]

The Vietnam Veterans Memorial

In the years after the war, a Vietnam veteran named Jan Scruggs called for a national monument to honor Vietnam veterans. For the first time in its history, America had pulled out of a major war, and Vietnam vets had come home to a weary and bitter nation. There were no victory parades for them and few honors. Scruggs felt that a monument was needed to remember the sacrifice of nearly sixty thousand Americans, regardless of the war's outcome or how unpopular it had been. He and other vets started a Vietnam Veterans Memorial Fund, and in 1980, President Jimmy Carter signed a bill setting aside a location on the National Mall in the nation's capital for the memorial.

The fund paid for an open competition to design the new memorial. Out of 1,421 entries, the winning design was submitted by a young architecture student named Maya Lin. In her design, two black marble walls form an extended V on which the names of the more than fifty-eight thousand soldiers killed or missing in action in Vietnam are engraved.

Lin has said that she did no research into the Vietnam War before creating her design because she did not want to be influenced by politics. Instead,

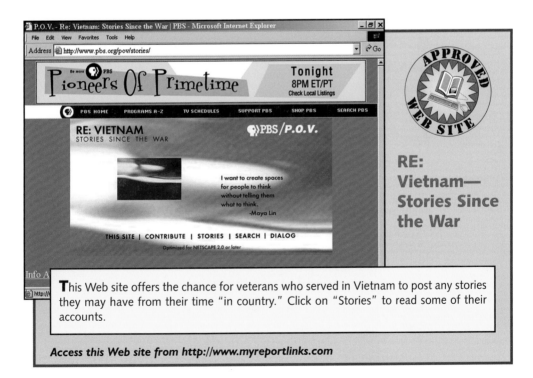

This Web site offers the chance for veterans who served in Vietnam to post any stories they may have from their time "in country." Click on "Stories" to read some of their accounts.

Access this Web site from http://www.myreportlinks.com

she wanted the simple structure to reflect the mourning of the nation. The simplicity allowed people to experience the memorial in their own ways. "I was trying to come to some understanding of mourning and grieving," Lin remarked. "We as Americans are more afraid of death and aging than many other cultures—we don't want to accept it or deal with it. So when the memorial was under construction, the reaction was, 'It's too subtle, it's too personal, I don't get this, it won't work.' But the fact that it does work may say something about what the American public really needed."[5]

At first, veterans groups and some members of Congress protested the memorial's design. In the *New York Times,* Vietnam veteran Thomas Carhart wrote that the memorial was "a black gash of shame and sorrow, hacked into the national visage that is the Mall."[6]

▶ Critics Come Around

Soon, however, many critics of the Wall—as the memorial has come to be called—came to appreciate and even love Lin's elegant and moving design. In November 1982, more than 150,000 veterans traveled to Washington, D.C., for the memorial's dedication. Some critics, though, still wanted a traditional statue added to the memorial, showing American soldiers. In 1984, a statue crafted by sculptor Frederick Hart, depicting a small group of foot soldiers staring toward the Wall, was dedicated.

Boosted by two Marines, a member of the Vietnam Vets Motorcycle Club traces the name of a friend's son on the Wall.

In 1993, a statue honoring women's service in the war, designed by Glenna Goodacre, was erected not far away.

Today, the Wall is one of the most visited monuments in Washington, D.C., drawing about 4 million visitors each year. The National Park Service has collected tens of thousands of artifacts left there by visitors, including service medals, combat boots, flowers, and family photographs. Some of these are displayed in the Smithsonian Institution.

▷ Trade With Vietnam

Although the Wall allowed millions of Americans to make peace with the Vietnam War, the United States government did not make a major step toward lasting peace with Vietnam until the 1990s. In 1994, President Bill Clinton lifted the trade embargo on Vietnam. Because the United States government did not wish to benefit the Communist government of Vietnam, it had placed an embargo—or barrier—on any trade with Vietnam. By the 1990s, however, Clinton noted that the Vietnamese government had been cooperating with the United States on several important issues. Primarily, Vietnamese officials had been helping the United States to locate American MIAs, still missing two decades after the war. The Vietnamese were also working closely with neighboring Laos, where many American lives had been lost as well. In the process, many soldiers' remains were returned to their families for a proper burial.

On July 11, 1995, President Clinton announced that the administration had normalized diplomatic relationships with Vietnam:

Let me emphasize, normalization of our relations with Vietnam is not the end of our effort [to find missing soldiers]. . . . We will keep working until we get all the answers we can. Our strategy is working. Normalization of relations is the next appropriate step. With this new relationship, we will be able to make more progress. . . .

I am proud to be joined in this view by distinguished veterans of the Vietnam War. They served their country bravely. They are of different [political] parties. A generation ago they had different judgments about the war which divided us so deeply. But today they are of a single mind. They agree that the

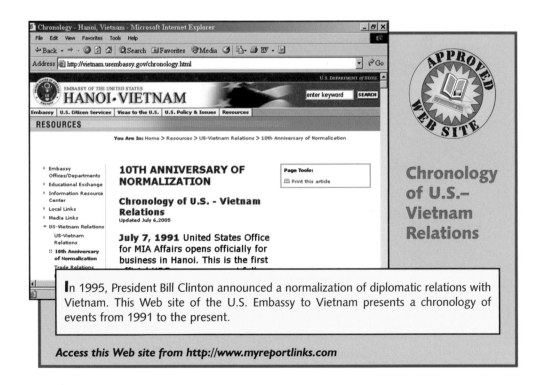

In 1995, President Bill Clinton announced a normalization of diplomatic relations with Vietnam. This Web site of the U.S. Embassy to Vietnam presents a chronology of events from 1991 to the present.

Access this Web site from http://www.myreportlinks.com

time has come for America to move forward on Vietnam.[7]

The Vietnam War Lingers

In the hard-fought presidential election of 2004, however, the Vietnam War became a major issue again, nearly three decades after the fall of Saigon. Critics of the Democratic presidential nominee, Senator John Kerry, charged that he may have over-stated the injuries he suffered during his two tours of duty in Vietnam. Some Vietnam veterans also felt betrayed by Kerry, because he had spoken out against the war after he returned.

Critics of the incumbent Republican president, George W. Bush, were just as harsh. They accused Bush of avoiding combat during the war by staying stateside and serving in the National Guard. Some people claimed that the president had skipped out on his Guard duties altogether at various times. When George Bush won reelection in November 2004 by a slim margin, some observers noted that the criticisms of John Kerry had probably been more damaging to the candidate's chances of becoming president.

The elections proved that the bitter divisions that existed during the Vietnam War still exist today. It may be a long time before the United States and Vietnam can completely recover from their war wounds. But they can try.

At his 1995 announcement about normalizing trade, President Clinton made an appeal for peace and resolution. "Whatever we may think about the political decisions of the Vietnam era, the brave Americans who fought and died there had noble motives," he said. ". . . This step will also help our own country to move forward on an issue that has separated Americans from one another for too long now. Let the future be our destination." In closing, Clinton used some of the same words from the Bible that Pete Seeger had put to music so memorably three decades ago: "Let this moment, in the words of the Scripture, be a time to heal and a time to build."[8]

Report Links

The Internet sites described below can be accessed at http://www.myreportlinks.com

▶**Vietnam Online**
Editor's Choice This PBS site offers in-depth information on the Vietnam War.

▶**Veterans History Project**
Editor's Choice This Library of Congress site presents first-person accounts of American veterans.

▶**The Wars for Viet Nam: 1945 to 1975**
Editor's Choice Take a closer look at the Vietnam War on this Web site.

▶**Battlefield: Vietnam**
Editor's Choice This Web site provides a look at battles of the war in Vietnam.

▶*American Experience—War Letters*
Editor's Choice Read letters written by American soldiers who served in Vietnam.

▶**Vietnam: 1954–1968**
Editor's Choice Learn about the fight against communism and North Vietnam.

▶**About the Vietnam War**
This university site offers a cultural perspective on the Vietnam War.

▶**The Air War in Vietnam**
Read about the use of air power in the Vietnam War.

▶*American Experience: Two Days in October*
This PBS site examines two days in 1967 that divided Americans at home and at war.

▶**Another Vietnam**
View photographs of the Vietnam War taken by the North Vietnamese.

▶**The Avalon Project: The Tonkin Gulf Incident**
Read President Lyndon Johnson's message to Congress about Vietnam and the resulting resolution.

▶**Chronology of U.S.–Vietnam Relations**
Learn about the path leading to diplomatic relations between the United States and Vietnam.

▶**Communist Propaganda From North Vietnam Project**
View photographs depicting the war effort in North Vietnam.

▶**A Different War**
The *New York Times* looks at Vietnam in 2000, twenty-five years after the last Americans left Saigon.

▶**Digitized Primary American History Sources**
View a collection of primary sources of American history.

Report Links

The Internet sites described below can be accessed at http://www.myreportlinks.com

▶**The Fall of Saigon**
Learn about the fall of Saigon from the archives of the *New York Times*.

▶**Ho Chi Minh**
Learn about North Vietnam's leader, Ho Chi Minh.

▶**In Pictures: Fall of Saigon**
Images of the fall of Saigon are presented at this BBC Web site.

▶**Lyndon Baines Johnson Library and Museum**
View online collections and exhibits of the Lyndon Baines Johnson Library and Museum.

▶**Maps: The Vietnam War**
Ohio State University presents a collection of maps from the Vietnam War era.

▶**Martin Luther King: Beyond Vietnam—A Time to Break Silence**
Martin Luther King, Jr., speaks out against the Vietnam War.

▶**RE: Vietnam—Stories Since the War**
Read personal stories from soldiers who served in Vietnam.

▶**Research in Military Records: Vietnam War**
This site provides links to military records of United States soldiers in Vietnam.

▶**Songs of Americans in the Vietnam War**
Read more about the music of the war, including songs created by the soldiers themselves.

▶**United States Military Academy: Vietnam War**
View battle maps from different periods of the Vietnam War.

▶**Vietnam Passage: Journeys From War to Peace**
The lives of six Vietnamese people during the war are examined at this PBS site.

▶**The Vietnam Project**
A virtual Vietnam archive is offered on the Web site for Texas Tech University.

▶**Vietnam: The Music of Protest**
Learn more about protest music of the Vietnam War era.

▶**Vietnam Veterans Oral History and Folklore Project**
Learn about an ongoing project to find and collect songs of soldiers.

▶**Vietnam: Yesterday and Today**
A university professor provides an online resource of the Vietnam War era.

ammo—Short for *ammunition,* explosive devices such as grenades and bombs.

artillery—Weapons such as guns and rockets; also a unit of the army that is armed with such weapons.

base camp—A semipermanent field headquarters for a unit.

battalion—Infantry and artillery units of the Army and Marines, commanded by lieutenant colonels.

casualties—Those who are wounded or lose their lives during war, including those unaccounted for (prisoners of war and missing in action).

Charlie—Slang term for Vietcong (from the phonetic terms for VC, "Victor Charlie").

decamp—To break camp.

domino theory—A political theory that took hold in 1950s America. It stated that communism in one nation would spread to neighboring nations, especially in the case of Vietnam.

draft—The process of selecting individuals for compulsory military service.

enlisted men—Those serving in the military who rank below commissioned officers.

escalate—To grow in intensity or duration.

flashbacks—Brief remembrances of past events; long after the war, Vietnam veterans suffered flashbacks of particularly horrific events they had seen or been involved in.

foxhole—A pit dug quickly to hide from the enemy.

frag—A common term for a grenade.

gook—An offensive term describing Asians used by American soldiers to describe the North Vietnamese and Vietcong.

grunt—Popular name for a foot soldier or infantryman in Vietnam.

guerrilla warfare—Unconventional tactics used in war, such as harassment, hiding, and ambush.

imperialists—Term used by Communist party members of North Vietnam to refer to the United States' aggression in fighting a war on Vietnamese soil.

in country—Term used to refer to Vietnam by those serving there.

infantry—Soldiers who fight on foot; also a unit of soldiers who fight this way.

irregulars—Individuals who were armed and fought but were not regular members of the army or police.

P.O.W.—Prisoner of war.

platoon—A military unit of about 45 men belonging to a company. Platoons were commanded by lieutenants.

provisional—Temporary.

search and destroy—Military missions to find and destroy enemy forces.

Tet—The Vietnamese New Year, based on the lunar calendar.

Vietcong or VC—Communist forces in Vietnam.

Chapter 1. Dispatches From the Tet Offensive

1. Bernard Edelman, ed., *Dear America: Letters Home from Vietnam* (New York: Norton, 1985), p. 72.

2. Bill Adler, ed., *Letters from Vietnam* (New York: Presidio Press/Ballantine Books, 2003), pp. 60–61.

3. Ibid., pp. 12–13.

4. John C. McManus, "Battleground Saigon," *Vietnam,* February 2004, <www.historynet.com/vn/blbattlegroundsaigon/index.html> (October 15, 2005).

5. Ibid.

Chapter 2. A Brief History of the Vietnam War

1. Stanley Karnow, *Vietnam: A History,* second edition (New York: Penguin Books, 1997), p. 11.

2. Tad Bartimus, et. al, *War Torn: Stories of War from the Women Reporters Who Covered Vietnam* (New York: Random House, 2002), p. 121. Copyright © Edith Lederer. Reproduced with permission of copyright holder.

3. Eisenhower National Historic Site, "The Quotable Quotes of Dwight D. Eisenhower," n.d., <http://www.nps.gov/eise/quotes.htm> (October 15, 2005).

4. Joint Resolution of Congress H.J. RES 1145 August 7, 1964, from the United States Department of State Bulletin, August 24, 1964, as quoted in the Avalon Project at Yale Law School, "The Tonkin Gulf Incident; 1964," <http://www.yale.edu/lawweb/avalon/tonkin-g.htm> (September 16, 2005).

5. *The Pentagon Papers,* Gravel Edition, vol. 4 (Boston: Beacon Press, 1971), pp. 632–633; <www.mtholyoke.edu/acad/intrel/pentagon4/ps2.htm> (October 12, 2005).

6. Transcript of interview with William Westmoreland, CNN's *Cold War* series, "Episode 11: Vietnam 1954–968," n.d., <www.cnn.com/SPECIALS/cold.war/episodes/11/interviews/westmoreland/> (October 12, 2005).

7. Karnow, p. 669.

8. R.W. Apple, Jr., "Looking at U.S. Role in Vietnam," The *New York Times* Online Vietnam War Archive, April 30, 1975, <www.nytimes.com/library/world/asia/043075vietnam-us-rwa.html> (October 15, 2005).

Chapter 3. Soldiers' Stories: The Words of Americans and the South Vietnamese

1. Stanley Karnow, *Vietnam: A History,* second edition (New York: Penguin Books, 1997), p. 481.

2. Ibid.

3. Ibid.

4. Bernard Edelman, ed., *Dear America: Letters Home from Vietnam* (New York: Norton, 1985), p. 51.

5. Khanh Truong, "Memory of a Paratrooper," Vietnam Online: An Online Companion to *Vietnam: A Television History,* n.d., <www.pbs.org/wgbh/amex/vietnam/reflect/truong.html> (January 10, 2006).

6. Wallace Terry, *Bloods: An Oral History of the Vietnam War by Black Veterans* (New York: Random House, 1984), pp. 4–5. Reprinted with permission of copyright holder.

7. Ibid., pp. 5–6.

8. Ibid., p. 6.

9. Edelman, pp. 130–131.

10. Ibid., pp. 80–81.

11. Ibid., pp. 65–66.

12. Bill Adler, ed., *Letters from Vietnam* (New York: Presidio Press/Ballantine Books, 2003), p. 201.

13. Edelman, p. 212.

14. Ibid., p. 274.

15. Adler, pp. 167–168.

16. Ibid., pp. 193–194.

17. Edelman, pp. 111–113.

18. Ibid., p. 122.

19. Ibid., p. 245.

Chapter 4. Soldiers' Stories: The Words of the North Vietnamese

1. General Van Tien Dung, translated by John Spragens, Jr., *Our Great Spring Victory: An Account of the Liberation of South Vietnam* (New York and London: Monthly Review Press, 1977), p. 209.

2. Stanley Karnow, *Vietnam: A History,* second edition (New York: Penguin Books, 1997), p. 417.

3. Ibid.

4. Ibid., p. 470.

5. Ibid., p. 473.

6. Various authors, *Letters from South Vietnam* (Hanoi: Foreign Languages Publishing House, 1963), pp. 78, 81.

7. Karnow, p. 557.

8. Ibid.

9. Ibid., p. 558.

10. Karen Gottschang Turner, with Phan Thanh Hao, *Even the Women Must Fight: Memories of War from North Vietnam* (New York: Wiley, 1998), p. 120.

11. Ibid., p. 121.

12. Ibid., p. 148.

13. Dung, p. 232.

14. Ibid., p. 246.

Chapter 5. Dreaming of Peace:
   Other Voices Speak Out

1. Bill Adler, ed., *Letters from Vietnam* (New York: Presidio Press/Ballantine Books, 2003), pp. 85–87.

2. Winnie Smith, *American Daughter Gone to War* (New York: William Morrow & Company, 1992), p. 44.

3. Ibid., p. 119.

4. Ibid., p. 332.

5. Topsy Gregory, ed., *Dear Wisconsin . . . Love, Vietnam* (Self-published by Topsy Gregory, Big Ben, Wis., 1996), p. 13.

6. Ibid., pp. 26–27.

7. Ibid., pp. 80–81.

8. Ibid., p. 117.

9. Christian Langworthy, "An Amerasian Childhood in Da Nang," PBS; *American Experience: Vietnam Online,* n.d., <www.pbs.org/wgbh/amex/vietnam/reflect/langworthy.html> (October 15, 2005).

10. William J. Brinker, "Oral History and the Vietnam War," *OAH Magazine of History,* p. 5, Spring 1997, <www.oah.org/pubs/magazine/oralhistory/brinker.pdf> (October 15, 2005). Copyright © Organization of American Historians. All rights reserved. Reprinted with permission.

11. Ibid.

12. David Lamb, *Vietnam, Now: A Reporter Returns* (New York: Public Affairs, 2002), p. 104.

Chapter 6. "Blowin' in the Wind": The War in Song

1. **We Gotta Get Out Of This Place,** Words and Music by Barry Mann and Cynthia Weil © 1965 (Renewed 1963) SCREEN GEMS-EMI MUSIC INC. All Rights Reserved. International Copyright Secured. Used by permission.

2. Creedence Clearwater Revival Web site, "Fortunate Son" lyrics, n.d., <www.creedence-online.net/lyrics/fortunate_son .php> (October 15, 2005). Reproduced with permission of copyright holder.

3. Bob Dylan Web site, "Masters of War" lyrics, n.d., <bobdylan.com/songs/masters.html> (October 15, 2005). MASTERS OF WAR Copyright © 1963 by Warner Bros. Inc. Copyright renewed 1991 by Special Rider Music. All rights reserved. International copyright secured. Reprinted by permission.

4. Bob Dylan Web site, "Blowin' in the Wind" lyrics, n.d., <bobdylan.com/songs/blowin.html> (October 15, 2005). BLOWIN' IN THE WIND Copyright © 1962 by Warner Bros. Inc. Copyright renewed 1990 by Special Rider Music. All rights reserved. International copyright secured. Reprinted by permission.

5. Pham Quang Tuan, ed., "Introduction to Pham Duy's 'Me Viet Nam,'" n.d., <www.tuanpham.org/EnglishLyricsFull .htm#MVN0> (October 15, 2005).

Chapter 7. Front Lines, Front Page: Press Coverage of the War

1. Tad Bartimus, et. al., *War Torn: Stories of War from the Women Reporters Who Covered Vietnam* (New York: Random House, 2002), p. 158. Copyright © Edith Lederer. Reproduced with permission of copyright holder.

2. David Lamb, *Vietnam, Now: A Reporter Returns* (New York: PublicAffairs, 2002), p. 9.

3. Ibid.

4. Stanley Karnow, *Vietnam: A History,* second edition (New York: Penguin Books, 1997), pp. 502–503.

5. James P. Pinkerton, "Bush Is More Like Churchill than Johnson," Newsday, April 1, 2003, p. A35.

6. Keyes Beech, "Westmoreland's Plight," *The Washington Post,* August 1, 1967, p. A13.

7. Bernard D. Nossiter, "Thousands of Students Protest War," *The Washington Post,* May 6, 1970, p. A1.

8. Walter Cronkite, "We Are Mired in Stalemate," CBS Evening News Broadcast, February 27, 1968, cited from *Reporting Vietnam: Part One: American Journalism 1959–1969* (1998), pp. 581–582, <www.digitalhistory.uh.edu/learning_history/vietnam/cronkite .cfm> (October 15, 2005).

9. Robin Groom, "Chronology: Vietnam in Context," *The Washington Post,* n.d., <www.washingtonpost.com/wp-srv/ national/longterm/vietnam/chronology.htm> (October 15, 2005). [The Johnson quote is often attributed in slightly different ways, with one of the most common quotes being "If I've lost Cronkite, I've lost middle America."]

Chapter 8. To Everything, There Is a Season

1. Paul Zollo, "Pete Seeger Reflects on His Legendary Songs," Grammy, January 7, 2005, available from <www.grammy .com/features/2005/0107_seeger.aspx> (October 15, 2005).

2. Roger McGuinn, "Tablature for Popular Byrds Tunes," n.d., <www.lyon.edu/webdata/users/kadler/public_html/rmcguinn/ tab_index.html> (October 15, 2005).

3. Hien Duc Do, *The Vietnamese Americans* (Westport, Conn.: Greenwood Press, 1999), p. 28. Reproduced with permission of Greenwood Publishing Group, Inc., Westport, Connecticut.

4. Susan Swanson, "Vietnamese Celebrate 'Women's Day' in Old and New Ways," *The Washington Post,* March 16, 1978, p. VA9.

5. Robert F. Howe, "Monumental Achievement," *Smithsonian,* vol. 33, no. 8, November 2002, <www.smithsonianmag.si .edu/smithsonian/issues02/nov02/pdf/smithsonian_november_2 002_monumental_achievement.pdf>(October 15, 2005).

6. Tom Carhart, "Insulting Vietnam Vets," The *New York Times,* October 24, 1981, p. 23.

7. President Bill Clinton, transcript, "Remarks by the President in Announcement on Normalization of Diplomatic Relations with Vietnam," The Clinton Library, July 11, 1995, <www .clintonlibrary.gov> (October 15, 2005).

8. Ibid.

Caputo, Philip. *Ten Thousand Days of Thunder: A History of the Vietnam War.* New York: Atheneum Books for Young Readers, 2005.

Galt, Margot Fortunato. *Stop This War!: American Protest of the Conflict in Vietnam.* Minneapolis: Lerner Publications, 2000.

Hillstrom, Kevin, and Laurie Collier Hillstrom. *Vietnam War: Primary Sources.* Detroit: U.X.L., 2001.

Levy, Debbie. *The Vietnam War.* Minneapolis: Lerner Publications, 2004.

Lindop, Edmund. *Dwight D. Eisenhower, John F. Kennedy, Lyndon B. Johnson.* New York: Twenty-First Century Books, 1996.

McCormick, Anita Louise. *The Vietnam Antiwar Movement in American History.* Berkeley Heights, N.J.: Enslow Publishers, Inc., 2000.

Philip, Neil, ed. *War and the Pity of War.* New York: Clarion Books, 1998.

Warren, Andrea. *Escape From Saigon: A Vietnam War Orphan Becomes an American Boy.* New York: Farrar, Straus and Giroux, 2004.

Young, Marilyn B., John J. Fitzgerald, and A. Tom Grunfeld. *The Vietnam War: A History in Documents.* New York: Oxford University Press, 2002.

A

accounts of war
American Red Cross
workers, 72–73, 76–78
American soldiers (*See*
American soldier
accounts.)
civilian (Vietnamese), 78–82
journalist, 18, 19–20, 43,
93–104
magazine, 96
media, North Vietnamese,
102–104
newspaper, 93–100
North Vietnamese
soldiers (*See* North
Vietnamese soldier
accounts.)
nurse's, 73–74
South Vietnamese
soldiers, 48, 58–59
television, 100–102
Tet Offensive, 52–53, 67–69
Vietnamese civilians, 78–82
A Company. *See* 1st Air
Cavalry Division.
African-American soldier
accounts, 49–51
Agent Orange, 7
"Ambush," 54
Amerasians in Vietnam, 78–80
*American Daughter Gone to
War* (Smith), 76
American Red Cross workers
accounts, 72–73, 76–78
American soldier accounts
home, thoughts of, 55–61
Tet offensive, 11–17
war in general, 44–55
An, Pham Xuan, 103–104
*Another Vietnam: Pictures of
the War from the Other
Side,* 103
antiwar protests. *See also*
songs of war.
history of, 7, 33
media coverage of, 98–100
and politics at home,
36–37, 39
quotes regarding, 56
anxiety, 47, 52, 57. *See also*
emotional issues; fear.

art and communism,
66–67, 90
assassinations, 25, 27, 36–37,
55, 77
Associated Press (AP), 94, 95

B

Baez, Joan, 87, 90
Banks, E. J., 45
Bao, Mr., 80
Beech, Keyes, 98
Bien Hoa, 12
"Big Red One," p. 73.
See also 1st Infantry
Division.
Binh Chanh, 16
"Blowin' in the Wind," 89–90
boat people, 107–108
bombings, secret, 7, 38–39
Bourne, Alan, 11–13
Browne, Malcolm, 95
Bush, George W., 114

C

Calley, William, 36, 98
Cambodia in Vietnamese
history
in antiwar protests, 100
bombing of, 7, 39
Special Forces actions in, 85
as supply route, 25
Camp Pendleton, 107
Cam Ranh Bay, 11, 13
Carhart, Thomas, 110
Carter, James, 109
casualties, 19, 98
Charlie Company, 11th
Brigade, Americal
Division, 36
children in the Vietnam War,
36, 60–61, 78
China in Vietnamese history,
6, 20, 23
civilian accounts
(Vietnamese), 78–82
Clinton, William J., 112–115
Cold War, 22
combat, nature of, 47–48
communism, 22, 23, 66–67
Country Joe & the Fish, 87
Creedence Clearwater
Revival, 87
Cronkite, Walter, 100–102
Cuban Missile Crisis, 26

D

Dai, Bao, 23
Da Nang
battle for, 31, 41
map site of, 8
media coverage of, 95–96
personal account of, 50
troop arrival in, 7
*Dear Wisconsin . . . Love,
Vietnam,* 77
Diem, Ngo Dinh, 6, 23, 25–27
Dien Bien Phu, 6, 21
Do, Tran, 64, 68–69
domino theory, 23
Donovan, Hedley, 96
Dung, Van Tiên, 62, 70–71
Duy, Pham, 90–92
Dylan, Bob, 88, 89

E

Easter Offensive, 7
Edwards, Reginald "Malik,"
49–51
Ehrhart, William, 46–47
Eisenhower, Dwight, 6,
23, 88
emotional issues, 57, 75–78.
See also anxiety; fear.
*Even the Women Must
Fight: Memories of War
from North Vietnam*
(Linh), 69

F

fear. *See also* anxiety;
emotional issues; short-
timer's syndrome.
of communism, 6, 23
in personal accounts,
5, 65, 75
and resistance, 66
in war experience, 17, 45,
57, 65
Ferguson, Roy, 60
1st Air Cavalry Division, 14,
31, 47
1st Infantry Division, 73
"Fortunate Son," 87–88
Fox, Cottrell, 13–14
France in Vietnamese history,
6, 20–21, 25

G

Geneva Conference in
  Vietnamese history,
  6, 9, 23, 25
Giap, Vo Nguyen, 67
Gibler, John, 16
Goodacre, Glenna, 112
Green Berets, 85, 86. *See also*
  Special Forces.
Gregory, Bridget, 76–78
Gulf of Tonkin incident,
  7, 28
Gulf of Tonkin Resolution, 7,
  28–30

H

Hagmann, John "Butch," 57
Halberstam, David, 95
Hanoi, North Vietnam
  bombing of, 7
  as capital, 25, 42
  and the fall of Saigon, 71
  in personal accounts, 98
  Western media in, 96
Hart, Frederick, 110
Hersh, Seymour, 98–99
Hess, Martha, 80
Ho Chi Minh. *See* Minh,
  Ho Chi.
Ho Chi Minh City (formerly
  Saigon), 42.
Ho Chi Minh Trail, 25, 64
home, thoughts of, 55–57
Hudson, F. Lee III, 15
Hue, battles for, 7, 8, 34,
  41, 69
Hung, Mai Van, 66

I

Ia Drang Valley, 7, 31
immigration, Vietnamese,
  107–108
Indiantown Gap, 107
Indochina War, 6, 21, 100
Iron Triangle, 32

J

Japan in Vietnamese
  history, 20
Johnson, Lyndon B.
  election of, 6, 37
  on importance of war, 28, 30
  media coverage of, 96–97,
    102

and Vietnamese
  politics, 32
war powers given to,
  7, 28
journalist accounts, 18, 19–20,
  43, 93–100

K

Karnow, Stanley, 18
Kazickas, Jurate, 19–20
Kennedy, John F., 6, 25–27
Kennedy, Robert F., 36, 55, 77
Kent State University killings,
  7, 39, 99–100
Kerry, John, 114
Khe Sanh, 19–20, 34–36,
  52–53
King, Martin Luther, Jr.
  as antiwar protester, 7, 33
  assassination of, 36, 55, 77
Kissinger, Henry, 39
Ky, Nguyen Cao, 32

L

Laird, Melvin, 38
Lamb, David, 95–96
Langworthy, Christian, 79–80.
  See also Phoung,
  Nguyen Van.
Laos in Vietnamese history
  invasion of, 6
  Special Forces actions
    in, 85
  as supply route, 25
  and US-Vietnamese
    relations, 112–113
Lederer, Edith, 94
Le Duc Tho, 39
Lennon, John, 87
Life magazine, 96
Lin, Maya, 109–110
Linh, Le Thi, 69–70
Long Binh, 12
Los Angeles Times, 95, 96

M

Macaulay, Kevin, 5, 52–53
magazine accounts, 96
Marine Corps, United States
  discrimination in, 49–51
  Vietcong, views of,
    50–51, 78
"Masters of War," 88–89
McCloud, William, 55–56

McInnes, Bruce, 60
McLeroy, James, 54
Mekong Delta, 25
military-industrial complex, 88
Minh, Ho Chi
  death of, 7
  as leader of Republic
    of North Vietnam,
    6, 9, 23
  legacy of, 70–71
  rise to power, 20–22
"Mother Vietnam," 90–92
My Lai massacre, 7, 36, 98–99

N

National Liberation Front. *See*
  Vietcong (VC).
newspaper accounts, 93–100
*New York Herald
  Tribune,* 97
New York Times, 93, 95,
  99, 110
Nhan Dan, 102
Nixon, Richard, 7, 25, 38–40,
  42–43
North Vietnamese
  media accounts, 102–104
  soldier's (American) views
    of, 50–51, 53–54,
    63–66, 78
  women, 64–66, 69–70
North Vietnamese soldier
  accounts
  of Americans, 62–63
  bombing operations, 63–66
  Tet offensive, 67–69
  war in general, 66–69
nurse's account, 73–74

O

199th Light Infantry
  Brigade, 11
Operation Cedar Falls, 32
Operation Rolling Thunder, 7,
  30–31
*Our Great Spring Victory: An
  Account of the Liberation of
  South Vietnam* (Dung), 62

P

Paul, Allen, 47–48
Peter, Paul and Mary, 87, 90

Phoung, Nguyen Van, 79–80.
   See also Langworthy,
   Christian.
Pinneker, J. G., 58–59

R

Red Cross workers accounts,
   72–73, 76–78
refugees, 107–108
Robinson, Bernard, 61
Robinson, George, 52
Russo, Frank, 61

S

Safer, Morley, 43
Saigon, South Vietnam, 11,
   40–42, 64, 70–71
Scruggs, Jan, 108–109
Seeger, Pete, 105, 115
Sheehan, Neil, 95
short-timer's syndrome, 57.
   See also emotional issues.
Smith, Mark, 47
Smith, Winnie, 73–76
soldiers, American
   accounts (*See* American
     soldier accounts.)
   described, 19, 46–47
   views on North Vietnamese,
     50–51, 53–54, 63–66, 78
Son, Trinh Cong, poem by, 82
songs of war
   about, 83–84
   fighting, 84–86
   "Mother Vietnam," 90–92
   peace and protest, 86–90
South Vietnamese soldier
   accounts, 48, 58–59
Soviet Union in Vietnamese
   history, 6, 22, 23, 26
Special Forces, 6, 85, 86. See
   also Green Berets.
Strickland, Hiram, 59
supply routes, 25, 32, 64

T

television accounts, 100–102
Tet Offensive
   history of, 7, 9–17, 34–35
   North Vietnamese soldier
     accounts, 67–69
   and peace movements,
     98, 101
   soldier accounts of, 52–53

staging of, 32
"The Ballad of the Green
   Berets," 85
*Then the Americans Came:
   Voices from Vietnam*
   (Hess), 80
Thieu, Nguyen Van, 7, 40
3rd Battalion, 7th Infantry
   Regiment, 16
Tho, Le Duc, 39
Tien, Nguyen-Van-, 58–59
Time magazine, 96,
   103, 104
Tra, Tran Van, 68
Truong, Khanh, 48
Truyen, Tran Thi, 64–66
"Turn! Turn! Turn!" 105

U

Uncle Ho. *See* Minh, Ho Chi.
United Press International
   (UPI), 94, 95
United States in Vietnamese
   history
   as advisors, 6–7, 22, 25–27
   as allies, 28–39
   postwar relations, 80–82,
     112–115
   refugees and, 107–108
USS *Maddox*, 7, 28

V

Vietcong (VC)
   as enemy, 19, 47,
     50–51, 78
   formation of, 25
   in the Tet Offensive,
     11–17, 34
Vietminh, 20, 21
Vietnamese civilian accounts,
   78–82
Vietnamization policy, 38
Vietnam Veterans Memorial, 7,
   57, 75, 108–112
Vietnam War
   battle sites, major, 8
   ending of, 39–40
   history of, 18–43
   map of, 24
   mourning, postwar, 105–107
   pivotal year of, 33–36
   and present-day politics,
     114–115
   time line, 6–7

W

Washington Post, 95, 98–100
Watergate, 42–43
"We Gotta Get Out of This
   Place," 86
Westmoreland, William C., 34,
   35, 68, 98
Weyand, Frederick, 17
women
   American, 72–76, 94
   civilian accounts, 78–82
   North Vietnamese, 64–66,
     69–70
   service, honoring, 112
Wonder, Stevie, 90

X

Xuan, Cau Ngoc, 80–82
Xuanloc, 41

Y

"Yankee Doodle," 83